A Memoir of AE

BUST OF AE BY JEROME CONNOR, c. 1930

A Memoir of AE

GEORGE WILLIAM RUSSELL

BY

John Eglinton

CORACLE PRESS

San Rafael, Ca

Second, Facsimile edition,
Coracle Press, 2008
First edition, Macmillan & Co. Ltd, 1937

For information, address:
Coracle Press, P.O. Box 151011
San Rafael, California 94915, USA

Library of Congress Cataloging-in-Publication Data

Eglinton, John, b. 1868.
A memoir of AE: George William Russell /
by John Eglinton. — 2nd, facsim. ed.
p. cm.
Originally published: London: Macmillan, 1937.
ISBN 978-1-59731-331-5 (alk. paper)
ISBN 978-1-59731-317-9 (pbk.: alk. paper)
1. Russell, George William, 1867–1935.
2. Poets, Irish—20th century—Biography. I. Title.

PR6035.U7Z7 2008
828'.912—dc22 [B]   2008021928

PREFACE

It is the men who have believed who are ultimately best remembered. The sincere assent of any mind to a religious interpretation of life is a memorable point in our human records. A man born with a spiritual perception has an advantage like that of those warriors of old who fought with supernatural weapons ; and the names of those poets whom we associate with any such perception assume in retrospect a growing effulgence amid names much more important in their day. What a name, for example, is that of Richard Rolle of Hampole, of Thomas Traherne, of Henry Vaughan, of William Blake. They seem to have owed little to their fellow-men, and their importance is altogether out of proportion to their technical accomplishment or to their authoritative standing in the development of thought or literature. It is possible that the name of George Russell will shine in the future with something of the light of these names and that his poems will continue to make him friends like those whom his personality attracted to him in life.

Let me then attempt a short life-record of this

A Memoir of AE

uncommon man, one of the most significant figures of modern Ireland. It has seemed to me a little strange that the task should have come round to me, as I was always a little outside his circle and we were even for some time estranged. But I was one of his early companions, and by a curious chance I was with him at the end.

How much I owe to those of AE's uncounted friends who have kindly made the writing of this Memoir possible, will be evident to the reader.

J. E.

September, 1937

LIST OF ILLUSTRATIONS

BUST OF AE. By Jerome Connor, c. 1930   *Frontispiece*
(*Reproduced by courtesy of the sculptor and of the photographer, J. H. Ardill, Dublin*)

GEORGE W. RUSSELL, c. 1890 . . *facing p.* 16

THE "COTTAGE-STUDIO" AT MARBLE HILL   ,,   114

AE ON THE SANDS BELOW MARBLE HILL . ,, 114

AE IN AMERICA . . . . ,, 194
(*Photograph by Zlata Llamas Coomaraswamy, New York*)

I

GEORGE WILLIAM RUSSELL was born in Lurgan, Co. Armagh, on the 10th April, 1867; 'so far as I can gather I was issued into outer things at about a quarter-past five in the afternoon'.[1] There is an entry of his baptism in Lurgan Parish Church, with the names of his parents, Thomas Elias and Mary Anne Russell. AE was not the man to care much about his pedigree, though on the father's side there were interesting connections; but there had been one member of the family who had done something disgraceful and was never mentioned by the father, and who proved, after the latter's death in the late 'nineties, to have been a certain Thomas Russell: AE liked to think that this was 'the man from nowhere', the friend of Wolfe Tone and Robert Emmet and one of the United Irishmen, who was executed in Downpatrick in 1803.[2] R. J. Frazer Hill, Headmaster of the Model School, Lurgan, writes: 'Thomas Elias was book-keeper in an old Quaker firm of cambric manufacturers,

[1] Letter to Clifford Bax, of uncertain date.
[2] The article in the *Dictionary of National Biography* shows, however, that there was no mystery about Thomas Russell's origins.

A Memoir of AE

and had married Mary Anne Armstrong, employed in a general store where he had previously been book-keeper ; she had been bred in the country near Lurgan. He is remembered by some of the old people as a man of striking appearance, gentle and cultured, and of deep religious convictions, attending the Parish Church in the mornings and the Primitive Methodist Church in the afternoons, and was much respected in the neighbourhood.[1] George was born in William Street, but soon after the family lived at the North Street entrance to Lord Lurgan's demesne in a cottage which was just inside the walls of the Park. In *Song and its Fountains* AE refers to an incident in his childhood at the age of four or five, when he strayed into a park and saw the clump of daffodils—evidently Lord Lurgan's demesne. George entered the Model School, where his elder brother and sister were already pupils, at the tender age of three years and ten months, and remained there for about seven years. The efficiency marks in the school records disclose the fact that even at that early age he showed literary gifts

[1] He was interested in music, for his relative, Miss Frances Calvert, possesses a copy of verses composed apparently by himself and written in a minute and beautiful hand, entitled 'Music Memoranda : Hints to help the Memory', showing technical knowledge. The taste was not transmitted to AE, who could not tell one tune from another.

A Memoir of AE

and was also good at drawing.'

According to the later philosophy of AE, the soul is a late arrival, entering or rising up in consciousness chiefly at the age of puberty, ' enriched with the garnered wisdom of countless lives ' : and he would probably have agreed with John Mitchel that hell rather than heaven lies about us in our infancy. ' I never felt a light in childhood which faded in manhood into the light of common day, nor do I believe that childhood is any nearer than age to this Being. If it were so, what would the spirit have to hope for after youth is gone?' (*Candle of Vision*). I remember him once pointing out a certain silent, rather ugly boy whom we both knew and saying, ' I was just like that ! ' In his autobiographical writings he is as indifferent to the influence of external events upon his life as India is to history. The outward scene disappears, and he attributes everything that happened to him in his slow development to the invisible agencies of the spirit-world. Almost the only recoverable incident of his childhood, which he mentions several times in his writings, and which was a revelation to the thoughtful boy of the heroic capacities of the human spirit, was the death of a woman in his neighbourhood, who, just before her death, wept because she was unable to rise and help a neighbour.

A Memoir of AE

When he was about ten years old there was an important family event. A friend of the family named Gardiner had become a partner in the firm of Craig and Gardiner in Dublin, and employment in this firm being offered to the elder Russell he was induced to remove to Dublin, where the family settled at 33 Emorville Road. Here no doubt George went to some school, and in 1880, just before he was thirteen, his name appears as a pupil in the Art School, which he attended thenceforth for a few months every year till 1900. His holidays were spent with an aunt in Armagh, and it is doubtless to this relative that he alludes in a letter (*c.* 1911) to St. John Ervine :

'May I say to you how much I liked *Mixed Marriage*. I thought your old Ulster mother the most human creature I ever saw on the Abbey stage. Yeats and Lady Gregory treat people in drama as Whistler treated his sitters, turning them into arrangements and harmonies, and I was very tired of their world. It may be because I am an Ulsterman and remember some grand Ulster women whom I never knew the like of in literature, until the old mother in *Mixed Marriage* nearly made me cry because she was so like a dear old relative of mine.'

A Memoir of AE

The earliest of his friends who now survive, Mrs. Coates, formerly Miss Carrie Rea, who lived near his aunt in Armagh, remembers him as a playmate with a great taste for drawing. 'I have a faint recollection of his sketching me as I hung to a tree-branch growing over a lake in Tynan Abbey and forgetting to push the boat under me. He once showed my sister the window from which he had been painting a little girl sitting for him on the opposite side of the street. It was similar to Mark Twain's story of the good physician : next morning she appeared with another little girl, and so on.' She remembers him joining in games, but he could hardly have been like other children, and it was 'while walking about the country roads near Armagh' that, as he tells us, a visionary faculty began to awaken in him.

He was already fifteen when he was sent to Rathmines School, then under Dr. Benson. Some years previously another boy, destined to eminence in the religious life of England, George Tyrrell, had been a pupil in the same school ; and AE used to say this much in praise of his old school, that 'it had at least produced two heretics'. But the two could hardly have been fellow-pupils. Russell's education was presumably of the 'commercial' order, for he never showed any knowledge

A Memoir of AE

of Greek or Latin, or of any foreign language. The Rev. Henry Chester Browne, who was his 'closest chum', writes : ' In school he was quickly recognised as having literary and artistic instincts of an order not usually found amongst boys, and he had to put up with a little playful ragging, from me as well as from others, in consequence. A lampoon of mine, done of him in 1883, describes him as "the special artist and literary critic of Rathmines College". We both left school about the same time in 1884, but remained the closest friends until I left Dublin in 1891. He and I, and another chum, Henry Goodwillie, took many long walks into the country together, and I was with him more than once when he was doing some of his earliest paintings on the banks of the Dodder. The sketch-book which he always carried with him, as well as a MS. book of his poems which he gave me, are still in my possession.'

In his home life we look in vain for anything like Blake's idealising affection for his brother Robert, and in *Song and its Fountains* he has written : ' I at last realised with a kind of anguish that I was becoming a solitary, that a gulf had widened between myself and normal human life, between myself and home and love, the things in which most find a rich content '. His sister died in 1884

A Memoir of AE

when he was seventeen, and in a letter to Miss Frances Calvert (1921) he mentions that he 'hardly remembers her'. And his own sons only heard by accident of the existence of the elder brother, who lived in Dublin and died some years before George, when they were already young men.

Russell's prose style, often employing Biblical quotation, and indeed his whole personality, bore traces of his pious up-bringing; yet in the first spiritual experiences he records, it is almost uncanny to note how little hold the teaching of his youth had taken of his mind. He delighted George Moore once by relating how, while staying with his aunt in Armagh, he left the house one day to 'think the whole thing out', and in five minutes had decided to defy a God who threatened him for 'doing things which he had never promised not to do'. If he is quite accurate in his account of these experiences, happening as he describes them years before he had heard of Theosophy, they are certainly remarkable. He had 'a vivid sense of a being seeking incarnation' within him. 'I was aged about sixteen or seventeen years when I, the slackest and least ideal of boys, with my life already made dark by those desires of body and heart with which we so soon learn to taint our youth, became aware of a mysterious life quickening within my life. Looking

A Memoir of AE

back, I know not of anything in friendship, anything I had read, to call this forth. It was, I thought, self-begotten. I began to be astonished with myself, for, walking along country roads, intense and passionate imaginations of another world, of an interior nature, began to overpower me.'[1] 'It was no angelic thing, pure and new from a foundry of souls, which sought embodiment, but a being stained with the dust and conflict of a long travel through time, carrying with it unsated desires, base and august, and, as I divined it, myriads of memories and a secret wisdom.'[2] This was the beginning of his doctrine of the Ancestral Self or Heavenly Man. It is possible that Russell, writing thus late in life, may have unconsciously mingled these transports with the first influences of Theosophy, but they seem to have come to him independently, and indeed seem hardly consistent in all respects with the Theosophic teaching.[3]

He began to paint his visions, and had been

---
[1] *The Candle of Vision.*   [2] *Song and its Fountains.*
[3] Even a firm Christian like Sir H. Rider Haggard had something of Russell's feeling about the soul. 'Like the Buddhists, I am strongly inclined to believe that the Personality which animates each of us is immeasurably ancient, having been forged in many fires, and that, as its past is immeasurable, so will its future be.' See *The Days of My Life*, vol. ii. ('A Note on Religion').

A Memoir of AE

attempting an ambitious series of pictures on the history of man, in one of which he ' tried to imagine the apparition in the Divine Mind of the idea of the Heavenly Man ', when, as he lay awake considering what legend he should write under the picture, ' something whispered to him " call it the Birth of AEon " '. Next day the entire myth ' incarnated in me as I walked along the roads near Armagh'. A fortnight later he was in Dublin, and while waiting one day in the National Library for an art journal he had asked for, his eye rested on a book lying open on the counter, and caught the word ' Aeon '. ' I trembled through my body. . . . I trembled because I was certain I had never heard the word before, and there rushed into my mind the thought of pre-existence, and that this was memory of the past.' He consulted the Librarian, who handed him Neander's *Church History*, and in the part about the Gnostics he found much congenial lore.

The mention of the Library is a reminder that he was at all times an omnivorous reader, especially of fiction. I remember what were still his favourites when I first knew him : Dumas was the chief, and he had a huge quarto of the six great novels, of which he knew every word ; George MacDonald ; Robert Buchanan's *God and the Man* : almost every-

A Memoir of AE

thing except Scott and Dickens. One would like to hear of his first encounters with the poets, with Blake and Shelley. A few weeks before his death, while lying ill in Bournemouth, he asked me to bring him a copy of Tennyson, and he then told me that when he was a boy his father had given him Tennyson's *Poems*, and that this was the first revelation to him of the art of poetry. Why could he not have told us a thing like this in *Song and its Fountains* ? It would have been more humanly interesting than the vague and inconsecutive evocations of memory in that strange record.

His father must have been puzzled what to do with him when he began to show as much interest in literature as in drawing and painting ; and was no more satisfied than Blake's father in a similar case with the direction his son's art was taking. And he did not at all approve of a certain tall lanky youth with whom his son had made friends in the Art School, one W. B. Yeats, in whose company the lad experienced the first stimulus of discerning admiration. For with Yeats arrived a new influence, which was to give rise to pain and division in more than one Protestant family besides the Russells.

A Memoir of AE

2

Probably there has never been in any country a period of literary activity which has not been preceded or accompanied by some stimulation of the religious interest. Anyone in search of this in Ireland at this time may find it if he looks for it, though he certainly will not find it in either the Catholic or the various Protestant religious bodies: he will find it, unless he disdains to look in that direction, in the ferment caused in the minds of a group of young men by the early activities of the Theosophical Movement in Dublin. The proof is, not only that there was no other religious movement in Ireland at this time, but that Yeats and Russell, who were to be the principal leaders of the Literary Revival, were closely associated with this one. The distinctive beliefs of Theosophy in Karma and Reincarnation hardened presently into the tenets of a dwindling sect: but what passed over from this enthusiasm into the minds of the youth of Ireland was the belief in the authoritative wisdom of ancient tradition and mythology. This was effected chiefly through the writings of Standish O'Grady, who peopled the Irish past with heroic figures and Druid sages, to whom Theosophy now added a more than literary significance. There was even a moment when some alarm at the ravages of this spiritual infection was expressed by members of the Catholic hierarchy; but with the growth of the Gaelic Movement, these vestiges of Pagan tradition were recognised as part of the rich inheritance of Irish Catholicism, and even a pious believer like P. H. Pearse could talk of the divine origin of the Cuchullin Saga. But this is looking too far ahead.

Ernest Boyd, in *Ireland's Literary Renaissance*, has told how the Theosophic Movement in Dublin arose out of a discussion in Dowden's house, at which Yeats was present, of a strange book which had just appeared, *Esoteric Buddhism*, by A. P. Sinnett. Yeats procured the book and passed it on to his friend Charles Johnston, one of a remarkable group of Yeats's old fellow-pupils at the High School, who also read it. The book offered the youthful mind an infinitely plausible theory of the soul, which convinced most of them for life of its truth. Johnston, a handsome, almost Olympic youth—son of the Orange Member of Parliament for Ballykillbeg—went over to London to interview the author, and returned to found a branch of the Theosophical Society in Dublin. Having joined it, there was not one of the new converts who did not feel that he belonged to the Faith of the future;

A Memoir of AE

nor was this faith in the least shaken by scandals about Madame Blavatsky—that teacher who, when attention was directed on her personality, withdrew it from scrutiny under a cloud of tricks and mockery. The teaching remained, and has hardly suffered by the unconventional character of the foundress. A similar moral ambiguity belonged to the personality of her American successor, W. Q. Judge, of whom AE wrote to Israel Regardie so late as 1932: 'Judge was the most impressive man I ever met, not by any air of dignity but simply from what he was'.

Membership of the inner circle implied acceptance of a rule of life which, conscientiously practised, left little room for any worldly ambition; and as none of these young men, besides Yeats and Russell, distinguished themselves specially in after life, it is probable that they now lost that incentive. Johnston, who had slightly scandalised his old companions by marrying Madame Blavatsky's niece, entered the Indian Civil Service, in which his career was mysteriously cut short (some said it was on account of his Russian wife), and he lived thenceforth a de-racinated life in the United States. As to Yeats, he went forward undiverted to play that part in his country's literature of which already he had a prevision. With Russell, whom Yeats had now brought into the movement from the Art School, it was different: should he renounce his dream of being an artist and a poet? For a time he hesitated. We have a glimpse of him in Katharine Tynan's Diary, December 1887: 'W. Y. brought a boy, George Russell, with him. Fond of mysticism, and extraordinarily interesting. Another William Blake!' 'He adored Willie Yeats and Charles Johnston.' In this circle he became acquainted with several of the new writers and artists.

It may be assumed that when Russell joined the Theosophical Society, of which he became at once an active member, he had turned his back on those ambitions in which Yeats had encouraged him. His father had obtained for him a promising situation in Guinness's Brewery; but, as he told Van Wyck Brooks in a letter written shortly before his death, 'I gave it up as my ethical sense was outraged, and then for about six years I lived with an income varying from thirty to sixty pounds, and was magnificently happy'. This refers to the clerkship in Pim's warehouse which was accepted by him in 1890 in the same spirit of renunciation.

One of his employers in Pim's still 'remembers him well as rather wild-looking but very business-like—a model employé and an example to others'. This part of his life was probably the most rich in human relations. He was happy and miserable, as youth contrives to be ; he was deep in the confidence of his fellow-clerks and shop-hands, and had some authority with them, for I remember a lady who had some business in the shop speaking with a little surprised satisfaction of the sharpness with which she had overheard him rebuking an assistant. He must already have been a wonder to them all, with his inexhaustible talk and amazing memory, his superior character, his interest in everybody's soul, his poetry and his turn for drawing—a gift which always commands respect. On the other hand, they were all under a certain overbearing superintendent towards whom Russell conceived a deep resentment : ' Sometimes I think I will blaze out at that man and scorch him up ', he would say to me, when I began to know him about this time ; and rankling memories of various humiliations were perhaps the beginning of his lifelong championship of the underdog.

Another of his superiors he found more sympathetic, a Miss Ellis, who was fond of talking about him in later-life, especially of how he had once come to her in her office, ' his Approbation Book in his hand ', and, while she was awaiting some business query, asked: 'Miss Ellis, have you ever really *seen* a fairy?' They took walks together after business hours, and she kept a sheet of paper on which he had written out passages from the Sacred Books—the same which he was to quote throughout his life.

He had left his father's house and now lived in the 'Lodge' of the Theosophical Society, 3 Upper Ely Place, a house 'run' by F. J. Dick, an engineer, and his pretty and delicate young wife, to whom AE refers in his poem 'How?':

> I must meet again
> That slender-lovely candle of the Lord,
> Wife of my friend, and unto all his friends
> A gentle sister.

No servant was kept, and my brother, H. M. Magee, who shared Russell's room, writes:

'I now burn with shame when I think of the menial duties we must have loftily left Mrs. Dick to carry out single-handed. Russell's great delight and consolation when he returned from Pim's was to study *The Secret Doctrine*, though I'm bound to say I don't remember seeing him "study" for long without breaking off for argument or discussion. I remember however the heartfelt way in which he told

GEORGE W. RUSSELL, c. 1890

A Memoir of AE

me how he was supported through the day's routine by the prospect of immersing himself in its pages—to him a contact with high Reality. The evenings would be taken up with discussion among the residents or visiting members; sometimes there were quite large meetings, at which Russell forced himself to become a fairly good speaker. He was always keenly intent on discovering what he conceived to be the nobler qualities concealed under often very unpromising outer characteristics of our little group, or of outsiders interested in the new Doctrine; and of course he idealised us all. On other evenings, Dick, who was a good pianist, would play Beethoven and Chopin for an hour or two. Russell of course had no appreciation of music, and would often be putting designs or even charcoal portraits on the walls. I don't remember much conversation when we retired: he would quickly bury himself in sleep.

'In those early days we (the unmarried ones) all hoped to become "Chelas" and expected to remain celibates, and were rather shocked to hear of Charles Johnston's marriage—even to a niece of Madame Blavatsky! Life at Ely Place was quite monastic. The urge of sex, natural to youngsters in their twenties, was hardly spoken of (except under the disguise of " Kama ") and was sternly suppressed. I am inclined to think, though he never gave a sign, that Russell himself was not immune. Someone (I forget who) told me of an unrequited attachment of his to a girl in Pim's, a common heartless creature apparently, who made fun of him behind his back.'

Russell's inner life at this time is illuminated by a series of letters to his early playmate in Armagh, Miss Carrie Rea (afterwards Mrs. Coates) ; they are written with a fervour in which there is no hint of romantic attachment.

'I do not think I will ever try to get either literary or artistic fame ; art and literature do not interest me now, only one thing interests me and that is life or truth. I want to become rather than to know. If I raise myself I raise the rest of the world so much, and if I fail I drag others down also. When this is once realised, when we know that in the inner world nothing but a verity convinces, nothing but an actual reality has force, we learn to cut away all that is superfluous, all minor interests. I do not believe that anyone could say they could never become a believer in this or that religion. If I thought that you had settled that you knew all truth already and did not wish to enquire further, I would simply leave you alone until I saw some chance of starting you on the search again. I do not want you to become a Theosophist so much as I want you to be always seeking for still higher ideals of life, to hold always an ear anxious for truth. I can have no friends outside those who are in earnest about life, *in terrible earnest*, though I may have many who do not hold my own views. Individuals are nothing to me, except in so far as they are manifestations of the divine life.'

As a Christian, his young friend feared Theosophy; she had literary ambition, and taking the part of a literary as well as a spiritual mentor, he finds books for her to read, at the same time, with the prudent craft of a father-confessor, indoctrinating her with the saving principles of Theosophy. He recommends Matthew Arnold:

' He seems to me to have two things absolutely indispensable to fine manhood, vitality and wisdom. By vitality I do not mean mere energy, but an inward consciousness of his true relations to the universe and to man, to the "eternal" which he feels within him, and its manifestation without. By his wisdom I do not mean his philosophy, metaphysics or learning, but those few precious sayings (a page or two would contain them, no man ever leaves more) which are the result of the conflict of the eternal and the transitory within him, and when the former has conquered. Goethe, Wordsworth, Emerson and Thoreau among moderns have something of this vitality and wisdom, but we can find all they have said and much more in the grand sacred books of the East. The *Bhagavad-gita* and the *Upanishads* contain such godlike fulness of wisdom on all things that I feel the authors must have looked with calm remembrance back through a thousand passionate lives, full of feverish strife for and with shadows, ere they could have written with such certainty of things which the soul feels to be sure. Yet we must not become onesided and blind to the outside world. I think spirituality without wisdom is almost as bad as utter materialism.'

In another letter he tells of the long day at Pim's:

'When one works nearly twelve hours a day, hard work, there is not much spirit left for other things. In spite of it all I am not a socialist. I think I have deepened in a good many things since last summer. What was worst to me in this overwork was what happens now and then in the hot room, the sudden flashes of recollection or looking out for a moment at the sunlight over the houses, golden white, the blue ether, the distance, the haze ; then it all comes over me, the sense of some divine thing missed, swift like a lightning flash incapable of analysis, only leaving a blurred impression on the mind as the lightning does on the retina of the eye.'

Russell finally overcame his pupil's hesitation, and she was to become one of those who shared his own feeling in later life, that there had been in him spiritual possibilities which were never fully realised.

3

I was not myself a Theosophist, but my friends were mostly of the faith, and I could hardly fail to know Russell, who at once took possession of me and always regarded me, I think, as a rather wayward spiritual disciple. I lived at Kingstown, and when the ' Lodge ' at Ely Place broke up (this is to anticipate a little) and he was living again with his parents at Seapoint, we fell into the habit of meeting regularly in Kill-o'-the-Grange churchyard on Sunday afternoons, where we were often joined by

A Memoir of AE

Charles Weekes. When Russell formed a habit he stuck to it. Thus when he called one Christmas Day, he received with an incredulous smile my plea of family obligations : people talked of tragedy in their lives, he said, but a true example of tragedy was the Christmas dinner ; and he turned away into the deserted country roads. Again, while returning late at night from my work at the National Library, I was liable to be called out of the train as it passed his station for a session in the churchyard, and I confess that sometimes, when I wanted to go home to bed, it was a relief when the train got past without my being summoned ; once I even hid, but I did not repeat this manœuvre after his solemn interrogation when we next met. Sometimes on holidays we took long walks. Russell at this period was liable to fits of profound depression, lasting several hours, during which he would not utter a word : then suddenly the cloud would lift, and the torrent of his talk break forth again.

His talk was certainly remarkable, and it was by no means limited to Theosophical subjects, but was often humorous and amusing ; he would narrate, for instance, funny incidents in Pim's. He infected us all with his own preference for the exuberant in literature, what he called 'prodigality'—Hugo,

A Memoir of AE

Dumas, Whitman—and for all impassioned personal utterance; and I remember, when one of Tennyson's last volumes came out, how he taught us to admire the 'angry old man' of the second 'Locksley Hall'. He seemed to have read everything, especially fiction and poetry, and to remember all he read, and I recollect his accepting a challenge to quote something from any poet we could name, from which he came off creditably. There was hardly any province of literature accessible to him which he had not at least looked into, to see if it had anything for him, though of English literature in general he wrote to me in an early letter, ' I see the great tree of English literature arising out of roast beef and watered with much rum and beer '. He disliked Shakspeare, whose tragedies he said were ' all about murders ' ; and Charles Lamb was a ' man who had written something about roast pig '. But he knew, for instance, the less-known writings of Edward FitzGerald (I fancy he would have been indifferent to the charm of the *Letters*). Again, he discovered that Byron's dramas were much better than they were supposed to be, and he often talked of them. He had discovered for himself one rather mysterious work, *The Dream of Ravan*, contributed by some unknown mystical writer to the *Dublin University Magazine* in the mid-

A Memoir of AE

nineteenth century, and had, I think, some share in suggesting its publication by the Theosophical Publishing Company in 1895; he was much interested in the speculation that the author was Browning's 'Waring' (Alfred Domett), in whose *Ranolf and Amalia* (1872) he found some resemblances, but later he gave up the idea when he consulted his friend Seumas O'Sullivan. In the early 'nineties, the romantic fantasies of Fiona Macleod began to appear, and excited his admiration. Sharp for some time corresponded with him in a slightly disguised hand as 'Fiona Macleod', and even when they became personally acquainted, AE continued to maintain that there was a real mystery: as was asserted by Sharp himself in a letter written to AE, 'to reach you after my death'.

It was the Theosophist in Russell rather than the Nationalist who murmured gently to me one day: 'Wouldn't it be a great thing to live to see the downfall of England?'—a remark which I remember roused in me a strong feeling of antipathy. It is curious to think how little interest any of us felt in national happenings. The event of 1891 was not, for Russell, the death of Parnell, but that of Madame Blavatsky; and in the following year the excited anticipations of Home Rule, the Belfast riots, etc., were hardly heeded in the preoccupation with those movements in the Theosophic world which led to a breach in the leadership, and incidentally to the visit of W. Q. Judge to Dublin (which by the way was Judge's native city). Judge left a deep impression on Russell: ' an inner exaltation, lasting several months, witnessed his power'. The Dublin Lodge became affiliated to the American leadership, disowning that of Mrs. Besant, and as part of its independent initiative a magazine was started, the *Irish Theosophist*, to which Russell began to contribute prose and verse. When in 1894 Judge's expulsion from the Society was demanded by Mrs. Besant, Russell addressed an ' open letter' *To the Fellows of the Theosophical Society* (his first separate publication, I think), an impassioned plea for his hero. He continued throughout his life to have a fondness for this mode of reaching his particular public.

It was as a talker that one chiefly thought of Russell, his painting being then in abeyance; and as to the verses which he crooned out to us in his mellow Northern accent, I had my own exaltations at this time over Goethe's *Gedichte*, and was a little disposed to agree with Charles Johnston, who remarked loftily of Russell's verses: ' My dear fellow, you have no notion how many people can write like that!' My opinion of the poems is different now; and already they had shown their power of taking possession of the mind, as only those poems do which issue out of the depths of conviction. The feeling for spiritual power and heroism which he communicated as a man found expression in his poems: his belief that whoever he was talking to was essentially a hero. This extraordinary young man, whose radiant inexhaustibility we took for granted, was part of the deepest life of all with whom he associated. I can still hear him, in Kill-o'-the-Grange churchyard, chanting:

We must pass like smoke, or live within the spirit's fire,
   For we can no more than smoke unto the flame return,

or
      Make of thy silence words to shake
      The long-enthroned kings of earth!

One could not think of Russell bringing round his spiritual wares to the publishers; but a bold idea suggested itself to Charles Weekes: he would turn publisher himself, and chiefly for the sake of publishing Russell's poems. To this proposal he encountered some resistance, but one day he announced to me that Russell had yielded. Weekes, a man of excellent taste, brought out the poems daintily in the Chiswick Press, and the success was

A Memoir of AE

greater than anyone expected; a second edition was almost immediately called for, and Weekes allowed himself the satisfaction of giving substance to the vanity of authorship with a cheque. 'It was a bargain for royalty,' writes this unusual publisher, 'on which AE won and I lost, for the trade return on eighteen-penny books is negligible unless the sale runs into thousands. I did not know that then!' It looked as if Irish literature might now have a publishing plant of its own, and it was an indication of the general interest aroused in the little firm of 'Whaley' when the great Mahaffy called at the dingy little office in Dawson Chambers to leave his card.

A compositor's difficulty in making out the word 'Aeon', with which Russell had signed an article, and which had been printed 'AE— ?', had suggested the pen-name now familiar to many who could not tell the poet's real name.[1] But the choice of the name was not accidental, and originated in the powerful impression left on Russell's mind by the early experience already recorded. In more than one of his poems—for example, in 'Ere I lose myself in the Vastness'—it is evident that he felt

[1] Russell afterwards adopted 'A.E.' as a more convenient form for general use, though he occasionally used the diphthong.

A Memoir of AE

himself to be not quite as other men who have lost sight of things of which he was assured. The dynamic idea of the poems is that man is divine, and so far equal with God. The recovery of this true estate, both for himself and for others, was AE's errand among men. In his poems (and this no doubt was his motive in consenting to publication) he might point the way 'Homeward'; and in one of his later books, *The Interpreters*, the conception of 'storming the Heavens' is expressed with unabated fervour. A mind to which the Gnostic myth of the 'proud Aeons', or the myths of the Titans and rebel angels, were a record of actual happenings in the abysses of time, may seem to some not altogether normal; but the same charge might be made against any mind which accepts literally any transcendental account of human origins. Ordinarily we call such accounts poetry or myth; but what is a myth? Or in what sense is a myth like one of Plato's 'true'? Is it not a resource of human intelligence through which, where history and science are impotent, essential happenings are shadowed forth? In this way the first chapter of Genesis may be 'truer' than Darwin's *Origin of Species*, and Plato's myth of the Cave a truer account of life than all our anthropology. Russell's mind was a natural habitant of that region of thought in which myths are 'true'. But his attempt to wrest the mythology of the race to a personal application produced a strain in his mind which is felt in the poems, and was ready, on any slackening of his incessant mental energy, to devastate his soul with sadness.

Let us then call Russell by his new name of AE. He had written verse from boyhood, and his old schoolfellow, the Rev. Henry Chester Browne of Dublin, still has the 'Sketch Book', lent by him to Russell to be filled in with sketches, which Russell had returned to him filled with poems. These range from boyish poems to some which appear in *Homeward*: one of the earliest must have been 'Heroism', on the incident of the dying woman which had so deeply impressed him.[1] In another

---

[1] These verses will be read by AE's admirers with an indulgent smile :

> 'Oh God, to think how soon each girlish limb
> Grew hard, and still with toil her eyes how dim
> With work from morn's first light to evening's grey,
> How swift the shuttle flew from day to day
> With fingers growing bonier, rest known not ;
> How bent the back grew o'er the garden plot ;
> Or in the field at work for her two boys.
> She had no time to think of selfish joys.
> They were her life, these two ; now they were grown,
> And toilers far for children of their own.

we find already the language of pure 'Fechnerism':

> She [the Earth] is wrapped in dreams divine;
> Eyes we are for her to see
> All her sister-planets shine
> Everyone as fair as she.

But in *Homeward* he has suddenly put away childish things, and the little volume really contained his essential poetic contribution. Later on he was to

> She filled their place with all the neighbours round.
> She had this habit still, perhaps she found
> In self-forgetfulness a secret joy,
> Strength for much weariness, and this was why
> Even in her pain she felt another's woe.
> It was a quarter of an hour or so
> Before she went: she wept that lying there
> She could not raise herself that she might share
> In nursing one less sick than she; her breath,
> So pitiful for him, was stilled by death.
> Oft have I read where many a poet sings
> In verse of famous and magic things,
> Of starlight clear, immortal drops of life,
> And whoso drinks has never any strife
> With death, nor sickness comes nor anything
> Which pains; and yet I never heard them sing
> That this elixir to their soul had brought
> Fullness or peace, true life thay had it not;
> But she, her tears showed, had true life, true breath,
> And they a shadow neither life nor death.'

acquire an elevated diction and technique which he could direct at will on devotional, speculative and on occasion (with much success) topical themes; but the freshness, conviction and spontaneity of *Homeward* were due to a combination of circumstances in his life which could not recur—the first excitement of Theosophy, companionship and probably some wistful love affairs, all coming together at the moment of youthful receptivity. As a poet, AE suffers from the limitation that his world is avowedly a Theosophical world ; nor does his belief in the divinity of Earth endow him with special insight into the life of nature. Yet even Dowden, who took little more than an amused interest in the vogue of Theosophy, could recognise a certain magnificence of statement in the poem he chose for special praise :

> The East was crowned with snow-cold bloom
> And hung with veils of pearly fleece :
> They died away into the gloom,
> Vistas of peace—and deeper peace.
>
> And earth and air and wave and fire
> In awe and breathless silence stood ;
> For One who passed into their choir
> Linked them in mystic brotherhood.

A Memoir of AE

> Twilight of amethyst, amid
> The few strange stars that lit the heights,
> Where was the secret spirit hid ?
> Where was Thy place, O Light of Lights ?
>
> The flame of Beauty far in space—
> Where rose the fire : in Thee ? in Me ?
> Which bowed the elemental race
> To adoration silently ?

A compliment which AE particularly appreciated was one from the American critic Stedman, who likened his verse to Emerson's. Another comparison was with Blake. Time alone will show whether AE as a poet deserves association with these almost sacred names. It is the task of AE's biographer to look for the man behind the poems, and it must be said that what one finds is less an endearing poetic personality like that of Blake than an immense spiritual claim :

> Each fire that in God's temple lit
> Burns fierce before the inner shrine,
> Dimmed as my fire drew near to it
> And darkened at the light of mine.

The man who uses such language is in danger ; but in Russell there were resources of character and talent which were to ensure his safety.

A Memoir of AE

4

The success of *Homeward* did not awaken in him any special literary ambition, and his 'hero' was now no longer W. B. Yeats or Charles Johnston, but Pryse, an American Theosophist who had brought over from London the original 'H. P. B. Press' and helped in bringing out the *Irish Theosophist*. Pryse was assisted by a Miss Violet North. In a letter of 1931 to A. E. S. Smythe of Toronto, Russell writes:

> 'The "grey visitor" [of the poem "How?" in *Vale*] was James M. Pryse, who first instructed me in magic, conjuring up pictures in the astral light, and holding them before my inner eyes so that I could see initiation scenes, the evolution of the astral from the physical, the movement of cells and forces in the body. He was one of the few members of the T. S. who knew things for himself and had a good deal of occult power. He was really rather a mysterious person, whose talk and writing had personal knowledge behind it.'

Outwardly, Pryse was a shabby, insignificant-looking little man, very Yankee in speech, as when he told of the sight of a wounded bird which in his

A Memoir of AE

youth had made him ' quit eatin' blood '. He took complete possession of Russell, and the influence appeared hypnotic : Pryse, for instance, would describe a circle round Russell and defy him to leave it without permission. He knew Greek, and instructed Russell in the esoteric meanings of the New Testament : he even directed Russell in poetry, though the latter may have had his doubts about Pryse's verse when Yeats referred to it impatiently as ' American jingle '. Pryse, on the other hand, with that reversion to the tone of the ' man in the street ' which mystics as well as artists affect in their criticism of one another, would say of Russell with a wry smile, ' He can do the sidereal all right ! ' They collaborated in a serial story in the *Irish Theosophist*, ' The Enchantment of Cuchullin ', with illustrations by Russell which they produced after a method of their own.

Russell's special psychic aptitude was found to lie in ' psychic vision ' ; and in the idea of the ' divinity of earth ', already native to his mind, and of an ' earth memory ', was found an explanation of the strange scenes and ' lordly ' figures which had hitherto unaccountably presented themselves to him in dream and reverie. They practised together the art of ' psychometrising ', through which ancient places were made to deliver up their secrets, and

A Memoir of AE

in Kilmashogue, under the Dublin Mountains, Russell discovered an ancient centre of magic to which he was often to lead his favoured disciples. The corollary of the 'divinity of Earth' was the specially sacred nature of the soil of Ireland, abounding in mysterious ruins, and readers of George Moore's *Hail and Farewell* are familiar with the picture at a later period of AE, interrupted by two Presbyterian clergymen while engaged in psychometrising the ruins of New Grange.

Moore, of course, was a rogue, and showed himself an adept in the art of Cervantes and Defoe rather than of Pryse and Russell, in the sympathetic veracity of his narrative. But, setting aside the questionable practice of 'psychometrising', it is more than a plausible speculation that the past is not wholly dead. The speculation is to be found in the most unexpected authors, as in Renan, who somewhere conceives of a point at which humanity will recover the memory of its total experience. In his essay on Fechner in *A Pluralistic Universe* William James writes of 'certain abnormal or supernormal facts': 'I doubt whether we shall ever understand some of them without using the very letter of Fechner's conception of a great reservoir in which the memories of Earth's inhabitants are pooled and preserved, and from which, when the threshold lowers or the valve opens, information ordinarily shut out leaks into the mind of exceptional individuals among us'. And Russell himself recalls in *The Candle of Vision* that ' an eminent thinker in science, Balfour Stewart, supposed of the aether that there was a continual transference of energy to it from the visible universe, and that the stored-up energy might form the basis of an immortal memory for man and nature '. The whole conception is persuasive to the mind, though it may be objected that we only thus explain the miracle of human consciousness by a greater miracle ; but we are gradually learning to distinguish between miracles which ' do not happen ' and those which initiate us into a world-order beyond our present comprehension. AE's was hardly a pure form of this idea, for it was mixed up with beliefs in all kinds of spiritual presences with which he held communion, on which a word must be said later. But he is certainly the poet of this idea ; and if William James is right in believing that it is in this direction that we must look for any satisfaction of the instinct in the human being to think of itself as immortal, it may well be that Russell will one day rank far higher as a poet than he does to-day.

Under Pryse's influence, then, he began to in-

A Memoir of AE

struct his disciples in a kind of national mysticism, of which some mention must be made, both on account of its indirect influence and because it entered into all his social and political theories. 'AEism' was really an attempt to supply the antiquity of Ireland with what it certainly seems to have lacked, a coherent system of transcendental belief; and on the strength of what seemed slender hints he disclosed to his disciples, in Ireland's remote past, a Druid priesthood acquainted with the secrets of nature, and a hierarchy of divine beings answering to the more clearly defined figures of Hindu and Greek mythology. To the Christian believer, faith is the evidence of things not seen, but AE's faith was in things that he had seen. If the Druid lore had vanished it was because it belonged to a spiritually privileged race which had superseded faith by sight and so never had occasion to commit its knowledge to writing. His visions and meditations—as may be read in *The Candle of Vision*—the work in which he has recorded his beliefs—brought him into direct communication with this august world of divine beings, who were not really withdrawn from existence, but out of a past still present in the Memory of Earth, continued to preside over the destinies of a favoured race. The persistence of the national claim, and the re-emergence of the Gaelic element in the modern degenerate English-speaking nation, were manifestations of their power. 'The pure Gael was the Ancestral Self.' When questioned as to the real existence of these beings, he seemed a little evasive: the subjective and the objective became as one talked with him interchangeable worlds. I remember once on an enchanted evening in Donegal saying to him, 'The fairies should be out to-night', and his reply, 'I could begin seeing them if I wanted to': which seemed almost a confession that they belonged to the world of imagination, However fantastic these ideas may seem when crudely stated, they did not seem so fantastic when he explained them. Stephen Gwynn, for instance, who once suggested to Russell that in the 'serrated lines of radiance' emanating from the head and back of the mystical figures in his paintings, Russell had been 'unconsciously directed by memory of the pictures of Red Indians', was impressed by the answer: 'No, it is the other way. Indians, being nearer to the primitive, constantly see these beings of another order, and to make their chiefs seem godlike, they invented this plumed ornament to copy the flaming aura that is about the gods.' Mr. Gwynn adds: 'F. S. Oliver said to me that of all the men he had met, AE was the most

A Memoir of AE

subtle, resourceful and resilient in argument '. Contact with his mind was a bracing experience. It was exciting to share his belief in a world full of mystery and magic; and the presence with us of a man whose faith never faltered was a possession for all his friends. He had no forbidding moods, no lapses from complete assurance. Most of us have to waste ourselves a good deal in a sceptical examination of what we are inclined to believe, finding, alas, that the more we inspect our fundamentals the more they seem to need inspection. Russell seemed freed from this necessity, and there was no companionable scepticism in his mind; but he would not admit that the soul can believe what is false. Religious souls, who were attracted by the radiant piety of his nature, never suspected how complete was his rejection of the props which sustained their own faith; as a believer he spoke to believers, and they were satisfied if a little bewildered. This freedom from wastage in his mind was a huge advantage. Consider what a transcendental belief implies in the mere freedom from worry! He grew prodigiously clever, more so year after year, with a power of getting things done which was helped by his private exercises in concentration.

A Memoir of AE

5

Many years after this period he wrote to Pryse :

'Painting is the only thing I have any real delight in doing. Nature intended me to be a painter. I was never taught. I went into an office, and wrote poetry. Then because I wrote good poetry I was taken from the office and sent out over the country to organise farmers. When I wrote one or two articles about farmers and their lives I was taken from organising and put to editing an agricultural paper. When I had learned to do this I was dragged into politics, and now I edit a weekly review dealing with politics, literature and economics.'

One of these transitions was at hand, and perhaps it was time, for he was now thirty, and his second volume of verse, *The Earth Breath*, published with Lane in 1897, showed no real expansion of poetic power. It enhanced his reputation, however, and no poet could have received more satisfying assurance that he had found fit readers. A distinguished lady wrote to him some years later, ' My inner life had its direction permanently changed by certain poems in *The Earth Breath* '. In these poems, Theosophy is less directly in evidence than in *Homeward*, and it is surprising how well AE fits into a Christian hymnary, as in *Songs of Praise* (Oxford University Press), where the beautiful verses, ' When the unquiet hours depart ', are quoted from this volume. Another poem, ' Janus ', was much admired by Yeats.

In the same year he produced two rather wild pamphlets, *The Awakening of the Fires* and *Priest or Hero ?*, written in something of the spirit which moved him, one Sunday afternoon on the esplanade at Bray, to mount the sea-wall and harangue the crowd. By a curious chance, Standish O'Grady, the man whose writings had worked in Russell's mind, so that he now experienced a sudden impulse to remind these respectable people of their heroic past, had been one of the guilty audience. Long afterwards, in a lecture delivered in the United States, AE recalls the incident :

> ' I think he hardly knew of the stir he was creating in the excitable minds of some of his juniors until he came home one day and said to his wife : " Meg, I heard to-day on the Esplanade of Bray a young man glorifying the ancient gods of Ireland ". That was myself, whom he saw then for the first time. I was ready for any

spiritual adventure, and I stood upon a wall in my young enthusiasm and told the people that the golden age was all about them, that the earth underfoot was sacred as Judea, and many other things which I think no street preacher said before or since.'

The two pamphlets were, needless to say, read only by a few Theosophists : contrary to his expectations, for he had written to Yeats : ' I will say things in fierce print to make people's hair stand up '. He had much to learn about Ireland, and he was now to enter on a long schooling.

Horace Plunkett had conceived of Ireland as a moral invalid, surrounded by witch-doctors and medicine men, themselves interested in maintaining their patient in the bad habits of centuries. His prescription was a drastic one, which even a national physician more gifted than he with magnetic authority would have found it difficult to enforce : it was nothing less than abstinence from politics for a generation, and concentration on a few plain rules which had worked wonders with other agricultural communities. It is to be remembered that in those days ' self-determination ' and ' economic independence ' had hardly yet been thought of, and a daemonically endowed leader with Plunkett's ideas

A Memoir of AE

might have gone far in directing the Irish destiny into new horizons. Nature, however, had not endowed him with any of the attributes of a popular leader ; some people called him a snob, and in fact the aristocratic aloofness which he shared with Parnell, and which the Irish are supposed to like in their great men, was not supplemented in him by anything of the romantic mystery and dramatic suddenness of the ' Uncrowned King '. His indifference to politics bewrayed him for a Unionist, just as his indifference to religion bewrayed him for a Protestant. Yet there was something royal in Plunkett, especially in his instinct for surrounding himself with loyal adherents, of whom the principal were the Jesuit Father Finlay, his Vizier, and his able and popular Deputy Anderson, whom with unerring vision he had called from employment as a land-agent and set in charge over his administration. His kingdom was not quite of this world, but his alliances extended into England and over the United States ; and that his house was a sort of court was made evident by his power of attracting talent. For though not himself what one would call an intellectual man, the most celebrated English writers, politicians and publicists were often his admiring guests.

But to initiate in Ireland a spirit entirely new : to

stir in the Irish farmer, if not a novel altruism, at least the motive of enlightened self-interest—Plunkett must have felt at times that the problem was nearly hopeless, since it was not merely a practical one, but belonged to a psychological field of activity in which he felt himself of no account. There was religion ; but he had no private call that way, nor was there any Father Mathew at that time in Ireland whom he could approach insinuatingly. He knew of course all about Bishop Grundtvig in Denmark, and the way in which a national feeling for the soil had been quickened in that country by an interest in native literature and folk-lore. Might not these new Gaelic and Irish Literary Movements have something in them which might begin to take the Irish mind off politics ? Yeats ? He had a talk with Yeats, but Yeats was not a man with whom Plunkett could enter into any common understanding, nor indeed one who would wish to wean Romantic Ireland from the pursuit of its chimeras. Yeats, however, had mentioned a young friend of his, practical and business-like, yet an artist, poet and visionary. An interview was arranged, but what passed at it I did not hear. Plunkett's kindly smile and persuasive personality must have counted for a good deal ; and Russell, we may be sure, unfolded his own ideals with eloquence and candour, and stipulated for entire freedom in pursuit of them. Briefly, after some deliberation, he accepted Plunkett's offer—a memorable decision: but it would never have been taken without Yeats, who had set his heart on Russell's acceptance. He knew better than anyone all of Russell's immense spiritual ambitions, and with delicate sympathy sought to persuade him that he would ' gradually absorb and harmonise ' the materials of his new experience, and that ' something new would grow out of it '.

Another motive may have influenced Russell in making this decision, though he allowed no one to suspect it, least of all Yeats, to whom he had recently written :

> 'I think I would break any woman's heart who ever happened to love me. She would find me as elusive as the Spirit itself. Perhaps it may be that I am half a woman inside. My reviewers could never make out whether AE was he or she. . . . The fact is I have I believe passed out of love and cannot write any true love poems.'

Judge then of Yeats's feelings when one morning in June of the following year (1898) he met Russell in the company of Violet North, and Russell said, ' By the way, I may as well tell you we are married ! ' It must be chronicled here also that the little circle

A Memoir of AE

of AE's disciples received the news with a certain misgiving : one had supposed that in his world there was neither marriage nor giving in marriage. He once remarked to me that he was 'proud of his love-poems', though it is hard to say what poems of his can be so named. Some of them are addressed to a woman, but a prohibitory vision of spiritual intercourse in the depths of the past always seems to intervene in the moment of transport ; and in one poem he exclaims, almost ungallantly :

> Though the dream of love may tire,
> In the ages long agone
> There were ruby hearts of fire—
> Ah, the daughters of the dawn !

Contrast AE in this respect with that great love-poet, his friend, with whom Love is still the flame which 'burnt Troy'. The marriage, however, proved a fortunate one for Russell, though his great principle that the claims of the family must not conflict with the claims of life bore a little hardly on his wife when he began to have engagements everywhere but at home. Possibly it was part of his controlling wisdom as well as her response to it, that this never seemed to bring trouble to the household. She shared in all his beliefs, and was valued on her own account by her husband's

A Memoir of AE

many visitors ; and she had her own life in bringing up their two sons. Yet Russell could hardly be called a domestic man, and he always seemed as much disengaged from family ties as Socrates amongst the young men of Athens. The words of George Moore in *Hail and Farewell* may be recalled :

' AE's life is in his ideas as much as Christ's, and I will avouch that his wife has never tried to come between him and his ideas. As much cannot be said of Mary, whom Christ had to reprove for trying to dissuade him from his mission, which he did on many occasions ; and if Christ had not chosen to remain a bachelor it is open to us to believe he would have chosen a Violet Russell rather than a Jane Carlyle.'

In joining Plunkett's movement, Russell became associated with a cause worthy of an idealist ; yet for a long time he was haunted by a misgiving, and indeed all his life there were moments when he doubted whether he had not at this time forsaken his true path. In the work to which they put him at first, that of organising the Raiffeisen banks throughout the country, his success was remarkable. ' Russell and those working under or beside him ', writes H. F. Norman, ' started about 250 of these banks, whose loans proved the salvation of thousands of small farmers.' Yet soon after entering on his new work he writes to Yeats :

' I feel all my old yearning to tramp through America come on me, and if I get a chance I think I will go. I seem to myself to be doing no good anyhow, and agricultural banks could be organised by anyone with a clear head and a capacity for smiling when he is bored. Look what you have drawn me into. I dine with P. P.'s every week. To-day I dine with a bishop. I give evidence before a money-lending commission ; I am asked to enquire the price of pigs. I have been forced to learn the different properties of manures. I have lived in country hotels, and been a thing apart from the " wholesome cheerful life of men " because I can't get drunk.'

And a letter to T. P. Gill is hardly that of an organiser whose whole heart was in his work :

' Here is another report. It was sacrilege to talk about banks as I did below Mount Nephin, which is largely stocked with gods, immortals and fairies. I am sure they felt civilisation was threatening them and fought vainly against it. I talked largely after the modern fashion about percentages, while the ancients of the skies pelted me with sleet. I was muffled up in two overcoats and defied the gods. I thought the gods would make a better fight and I have a half-disappointed feeling, for I believe we will have a bank. . . . I have spread snares in other districts and am watching the lines.'

Often the organisers encountered hardships and even danger in the remote districts into which they had to travel, as appears in R. A. Anderson's narrative, *With Horace Plunkett in Ireland*. I find a letter to myself, dated 'Belmullet, Christmas' [1897], in which Russell says:

'The drive from Ballina to Belmullet (40 miles on a frosty day from 2 P.M. to 10 o'clock) was a terrible experience. I was only saved from a frosty death by my dread of going into a bog. I heard the car went into one the night before, and drenched its wretched load of passengers. "The horses shy sometimes", I was calmly told as if it were nothing. A fat little country girl kept me warm part of the way and quoted local poetry to me and also faery yarns. But the rest of the way was a chill desolation.'

Mrs. Coates contributes a pretty story:

'One beautiful remembrance he had of a little boy who took him by the hand and led him over

A Memoir of AE

a mountain, presumably a short-cut to where he was to address a meeting. When the lecture was over, the little hand was again waiting for him, and together they retraced their steps in the darkness.'

He would hardly have gone on with the work had not the moral and idealistic aim of Plunkett's movement—to effect a change, which partook of the nature of a spiritual regeneration, in the Irish farmer—begun to take hold of him, and Plunkett soon had reason to hope that in enlisting the aid of Russell he had introduced a transforming influence into the Organisation. When spring begins, Ireland becomes a very different place, and Russell began to set off more hopefully in the mornings on his bicycle or on an ' outside car '. In a more cheerful letter to me he writes that public speaking, which at first had 'filled him with dreadful anticipations', was now no trouble to him, and that he could ' rattle off speeches with a careless fluency which is a marvel to myself'. Humanity in these remote districts needed a helping hand ; the arid life of the Irish countryside and country town called for an apostle ; and in talks at night with the parish priest or ' local magnate ' , with farmers and labourers, he laid up in his capacious memory a store of facts and observations which his gift of lucid exposition

A Memoir of AE

enabled him to use with effect in speech and writing. Soon he promised to become the inspired spokesman of the movement. Yeats, who had really been his good angel at this crisis of his life, expressed ' astonishment' at some speech which had been reported. In *The Irish Homestead*, the journal of Plunkett's Organisation, now edited by T. P. Gill, Russell began to display his formidable powers as a controversialist.

How much is implied in that simple phrase : He had found work which suited him. In Russell's case, a change as absolute as the passage of the mediaeval world into the modern happened when the dreams of youth were transformed into the energies of the practical idealist, and the eye of faith began to rest less on a distant past or future than on the complicated present, in which it discerned the rudiments of an ideal order of things. I do not suggest that his transcendental faith weakened; but now, when no single faculty that he possessed was unemployed, there was no longer any likelihood that he would go off to tramp America or retire as a Bhikku into a Burmese forest. He became the AE whom we knew, the ' perfect performer of action ', a man indeed nearer perfection, as it seemed to many, than any they had known. His remarkable conversational powers, and the range of his ideas and interests, impressed all kinds of distinguished visitors to Ireland whom he met at Plunkett's house, many of whom became his lifelong friends. Only his poems reveal a spiritual misgiving which, in all his new notoriety and presently fame, kept him unelated.

6

Mrs. K. A. Tingley, the American head of the Theosophical Society, or rather of the Point Loma Universal Brotherhood, had disapproved of Russell's decision to join Plunkett's Organisation, foreseeing probably the loss of a persuasive propagator of the faith. And in fact a year later, 1898, he withdrew from the Society. This meant no loss of faith in Theosophy, but a natural and common-sense claim for freedom. Theosophy may be said to have repeated, on a small scale, the early history of the Christian faith, in which, when the Founder had passed, the retention of His power and doctrine was claimed more and more exclusively by the Church. For AE the Society was nothing, apart from its inspired founders: in other words, he was a Protestant Theosophist. And it was in his personal understanding of Theosophy that he instructed a little group of followers in the Hermetic Society,

A Memoir of AE

founded in 1886 by Charles Johnston, and now revived. Over this Society he presided until 1933, during the early part of which period he became the spiritual inspirer of the Irish literary movement; and for the sacrosanctity which began to invest the shadowy figures of Irish mythology, AE was mainly responsible.

Meanwhile, Irish literature had become conscious of itself as a national movement, and controversies, in which Russell took part, arose as to its objects and ideals, particularly on the relation of the new dramatic movement to the ancient mythology. (*Literary Ideals in Ireland*, 1899. *Ideals in Ireland*, 1901.) One Sunday afternoon, in Kill-o'-the-Grange churchyard, he surprised me by reading out two acts of a play which he had written, *Deirdre*. They were printed in *The All Ireland Review*, and were read there by F. J. Fay, a little man with a sacred passion for elocution, who instantly saw his 'Irish National Dramatic Company' mouthing out the speeches. A play written with such facility could hardly be serious drama, yet its production by the Fays in April, 1902, along with Yeats's *Cathleen ni Houlihan*, proved a memorable event in the history of the new dramatic movement, of which, according to Ernest Boyd, it helped to 'determine the fate'. Russell himself designed the costumes and

A Memoir of AE

scenery, and his mellow northern accent was heard behind the scenes intoning the prophecies of Cathvah the Druid. The play struck a note which Yeats long endeavoured to maintain, until his dream of an Irish heroic drama was shattered by the demand which arose amongst his audiences for mere entertainment. As the future was to prove, the Irish Theatre was Yeats's affair and not Russell's, yet for some time Russell had as much authority as Yeats with the players, and a certain amount of asperity creeps into his letters to Yeats about the company's policy and constitution. Yeats grew irritated. The story does not concern us, as drama was to play no further part in Russell's life. But he retained his part in the councils of the Theatre, and must have had further thoughts of dramatic composition, for among his papers is the sketch of a comedy.

The Mask of Apollo (1904) is a little collection of mystical stories, reprinted from the *Irish Theosophist*, in which Celtic mythical figures alternate with Hindu and Greek. AE's standing as a poet of the Celtic Renascence was maintained by *The Divine Vision* (Macmillan, 1904). There is a profound spiritual melancholy in these poems, mostly on his constant theme of the dwindling of the cosmic consciousness to the flickering and half-lost ray of individual perception. One of them,

A Memoir of AE

'The Twilight of Earth', reads like a rejoinder to Shelley's exultant 'Chorus' in *Hellas*. Yeats used constantly to quote the line in 'Carrowmore' (which does not quite occur in the poem):

> Oh, the very sunlight's weary, and it's time to quit the plough.

But a little book which gave him more satisfaction than any of his own was *New Poems*, a small collection of verses written by young poets who would willingly have called themselves his disciples. The discovery and encouragement of new talent was not Yeats's strong point, and this part of the function of a leader of Irish literature was taken over almost completely by Russell, who loved nothing so much as to read a young poet's manuscript. Yeats and Moore indulged in gibes at 'Russell's flock', 'Russell's poultry-yard'. This time, however, Russell turned out to be right: the little book became quite famous and most of its authors were destined to independent distinction.

7

Of Russell's painting I speak under correction. Painting always seemed to me to be his most distinctive gift. Certainly he had a vision and a colour-world all his own, however much his blue-grey twilights may be a veil over incompetence in drawing and detail. But a Russell who had been to Paris, and acquired a conscientious mastery? 'What your pictures lack', George Moore used to tell him, ' is *quality* '—a word which always puzzled and rather nettled Russell. The fact that, as he told Pryse, he was happy only when painting, is hardly in itself a convincing proof of ' vocation '. May not a painter be as reluctant as a writer to begin work in the morning? But the notion of a born artist turning from art as a temptation is an impossible one. An artist or a poet, according to modern ideas, would be guilty of 'one wrong more to man, one more insult to God ' if he did not enter upon the path which lay clear before him. And in fact, if renunciation was what Russell was inclined to, his true path (always assuming that he was essentially a painter) would have lain through the lonely and often inglorious toil of the practice of art, in which he would have had to renounce the various activities which made up life for him. He would have recognised in the painter's brush the instrument put into his hand by Providence. Constable's proud saying ' I was born to be the landscape-painter of England ' is a different kind of

A Memoir of AE

statement from Russell's ' Nature intended me to be a painter '. Constable's failure would have been a true tragedy, but Russell's life is by no means a story of tragic failure. The conclusion is that though he had a real turn for painting, which might have been further trained and developed, he must have felt, with a certain regret, that the only course open to him was through the exercise of all his talents in the practical affairs of men. In painting he probably did what was in him to do, giving a great deal of pleasure to himself and to many who were glad to own his pictures, both on account of the pictures themselves and of their author. And, incidentally, he was able at all times to supplement his modest income by the sale of his pictures.[1]

George Moore once broke off a discussion on the subject by saying, ' Anyhow, there is no use in talking of Russell's pictures, for none of them will be left in twenty years '. I consulted on this point Professor Thomas Bodkin, who has very kindly sent me the following exhaustive note on the whole subject of Russell's painting :

' What follows is an account of a long talk I once had with AE in about the year 1914. It

[1] He told me once that in an average year he made about £150.

A Memoir of AE

arose because I thought at the time of writing a little book on living Irish painters, to include Hone, Jack Yeats, Orpen, and AE. But the project fell through, as Orpen objected vehemently to be associated in a book with either Jack Yeats or AE. Jack Yeats, anyhow in my opinion, is a greater artist than Orpen was, though perhaps not so accomplished technically.

'AE's earliest ambition was to become a painter; and when sixteen or seventeen he entered the Dublin Metropolitan School of Art and worked there at drawing from casts and the rest of the dull routine of the South Kensingtonian system. He was not promoted to drawing from the model and only remained in the school for six or seven months. W. B. Yeats, John Hughes and Oliver Sheppard were all pupils at the time. Hughes modelled in clay a fine bust of AE as a dreamy, sensitive youth with full, mobile lips and a broad brow. A plaster cast from this, coloured badly by AE himself, used to stand on the mantelpiece of the front sitting-room in 17 Rathgar Avenue.

'From the Metropolitan School, AE progressed to the school of the Royal Hibernian Academy, securing admission on the test of a small drawing. It was here that he first began to

A Memoir of AE

work in oils. He won a prize of a pound or two in some student competition. The teaching, in his opinion, was sadly inadequate and ineffective. He described it many years later in the evidence which he gave before the Royal Commission appointed in 1906 to consider the quality of art training then available in Ireland : " When I was an art student there ", said he, " I painted from the life. There were four Visitors who were academicians. One Visitor, Mr. Duffy, was an excellent landscape painter and I have a great admiration for his work. Another was Mr. Grey, who painted bulls and cows ; the third was Mr. William Osborne who painted cats and dogs, and the fourth was Sir Thomas Farrell who did not paint at all. These gentlemen, not one of whom painted figures, were put there to assist us in our work. They never put their fingers on the students' work, which was probably the best thing they could have done under the circumstances."

'The Metropolitan School and the Royal Hibernian Academy began and ended AE's formal training in pictorial art. When he left the latter it was to abandon oil painting for some twenty years. W. B. Yeats describes in *Reveries over Childhood and Youth* the beginning of AE's

A Memoir of AE

long divorce from the art : " One day he announced he was leaving the Art School because his will was so weak and the arts, or any other emotional pursuit, could but weaken it further ". George Moore in *Salve* tells the story as he says he heard it from Mr. Hughes : " He and AE were students together in the Art School in Dublin, and in a few weeks masters and students were alike amazed at AE's talent for drawing and composition : he sketched the naked model from sight with an ease that was unknown to them, and turning from the model he designed a great assembly of gods about the shores of the lake renowned in Celtic tradition. ' Compared with him we seemed at that time no more than miserable scratchers and soilers of paper.' Hughes' very words ! Yet, in spite of extraordinary fluency of expression, abundant inspiration, and the belief of the whole school that a great artist was in him, AE laid aside his brushes, determined not to pick them up again until he had mastered the besetting temptation that art presented at the moment. He feared it as a sort of self-indulgence which, if he allowed, would stilt his life."

' AE himself told me positively that, though he had always desired to be a painter, he gave up painting because his lack of means forced him to

A Memoir of AE

enter into some more paying, if less congenial, business. Though he abandoned the idea of making painting his profession, he never ceased entirely to paint. During the decade or so which he spent in Pim's warehouse, he produced numbers of little water colours, most of which must have long since disappeared. Katharine Tynan used to treasure a few. They were all mystic or symbolic in composition. He described to me one series of such drawings measuring about 6" × 4". It was no less ambitious than a poetic illustration of the earth's history from its beginning in chaos to its dissolution. Early man, a winged demigod, fought with monstrous flying reptiles. The last man of all "dwindled to a tiny figure" crouched with his family in the shadow of a normal human skull, which served him for habitation in the twilight of time. When he recommenced, about the year 1900, to paint in oils, he made a version of this lost drawing for Lord Dunsany.

' Another series of interest, done in what may be called the Pim period, were rough colour prints of Irish gods and spirits. A brother-mystic named Pryse who had some knowledge of printing, invented, in conjunction with AE, the manner of their production, from pewter plates etched in relief and coloured by hand. Mrs. George Coffey used to possess several of these, which are probably now in the ownership of her son, Diarmuid Coffey.

'When AE joined Plunkett and travelled for the Irish Agricultural Organisation Society all over the country, he began to sketch small landscapes at odd half-hours in hard, coloured chalks. Someone found him so employed at the Rosses in Sligo and recommended him to try pastels as being more suitable for his purpose. He adopted that advice and drew constantly with pastels for several years.

'In *Salve* George Moore describes a tour of three or four days' duration made with AE in the neighbourhood of Drogheda, New Grange and Dundalk. AE drew several landscapes during their wanderings and a pastel of Moore, which the sitter described as " clearly the work of one who has been with the gods, for in it my hair is hyacinthine and my eyes are full of holy light ". Moore did not retain his high opinion of AE as an artist; for many years before his death he was accustomed to refer to AE in tones of bitter contempt as " the Donegal Dauber ".

'Few of the pastels can now survive. They are perishable things and were done for the artist's

A Memoir of AE

purely personal pleasure, were never sold and never exhibited. Two or three used to hang in his own house. His work in the medium was not confined to landscape and occasional portraits. He delighted more to depict weird cosmogonies and hierarchies of ancient deities, plumed and crowned with light, ascending and descending in many-coloured spirals of flame, or sitting in council along dim ridges of starlit clouds.

'When, early in the present century, Count Casimir Markievicz settled in Dublin, he made the acquaintance of AE and persuaded him to paint more in oils and to join with the Countess and himself in an exhibition of oil paintings. This was the first of AE's annual exhibitions, and took place in the Leinster Lecture Hall in Molesworth Street in 1904. It proved to be an artistic and financial success, and AE continued to exhibit regularly, in varied company, for ten or twelve years more. At each of these exhibitions he showed from forty to sixty small paintings and sold them all at prices which tended gradually to increase slightly, but ranged between three and eight guineas. Other exhibitors who joined AE from time to time in these ventures were Frances Baker; W. J. Leech, R.H.A.; Kathleen Fox; Dermod O'Brien, P.R.H.A.; William Crampton

A Memoir of AE

Gore, R.H.A.; Beatrice Elvery (now Lady Glenavy), Eli Delbert Maybee, and Grace and Paul Henry.

'For the first few years these exhibitions were held in the Leinster Hall in Molesworth Street. After that they were transferred to the Mills Hall in Merrion Row. Only once did AE venture into the crowd of his fellow-artists: he showed three pictures at the Royal Hibernian Academy of 1905. They remained unsold during the exhibition: but shortly afterwards all three were disposed of for the prices asked at the Academy. One was bought by Lady Dudley, then Vice-reine of Ireland, the others by Lady Ardilaun. In the next year AE first came into contact with Hugh Lane, who greatly admired his work and bought several pictures for the Dublin Municipal Collection which he was then forming. AE told me that at one time every member of Mr. Asquith's Cabinet possessed specimens of his work.

'Among the masterpieces which Lane brought to Dublin in 1906 and 1907 were the first works by modern continental artists which AE had ever seen. He was enormously impressed by them, particularly by the Corots and Monticellis. In my opinion, he did his best work as a painter at this period. " On the Rooftops " and " The Winged Horse ", now to be seen in the Dublin Municipal Gallery, show not only the imagination which was always present in his work, but also a power of composition and a technical competence which he sometimes lacked. In later life AE said to me that he would like to replace some of the pictures which he sold to Lane by more recent examples of his art; but I think this would probably have been to the detriment of his reputation.

' He regarded his painting as a minor activity of his life : and only worked at it, as a rule, on Sunday mornings and during his annual month's holiday in Donegal. From this holiday he was accustomed to bring back every year about thirty pictures. He was an amazingly rapid executant. In 1914 I spent a week-end with James Stephens and himself at Virginia, Co. Cavan, and was enabled to study his method of work. We went one morning together into the woods of Lord Headfort's demesne. AE selected a view-point, set up a little portable easel on which he placed his canvas, and opened one of the smallest and, certainly, the dirtiest paint-box which I have ever seen. His palette was clotted with old, dried pigment ; his brushes were in a lamentable state.

A Memoir of AE

Without making any preliminary drawing he started to paint the scene before him. The result bore little or no resemblance to his model; but was yet an extraordinarily beautiful rendering of a sunlit glade. Before he had time to finish it we were all expelled by one of his Lordship's keepers. That did not prevent AE from finishing the picture afterwards at his leisure in Rathgar.

' His knowledge of the technique of his art was slight and, as a result, some of his pictures have deteriorated. He would occasionally start to paint a sunlit scene and his vision would alter as the work proceeded, till the final result was as likely as not to be a nocturne. Consequently, the layers of paint superimposed upon each other without having been given time to dry out, tended to go opaque and to crack. The only medium he used was turpentine, which, when used to excess, also induces cracks and fissures in the pigment. He never varnished his pictures, with one exception. This happened when, at the request of Sir Horace Plunkett, Mr. Dermod O'Brien and myself were commissioned to buy a few pictures by modern Irish artists for the University of Wisconsin. Among our acquisitions was an unusually large painting by AE. As the paint surface was dull, I suggested that he should varnish it. He did so by smearing varnish on it in criss-cross strokes with a stiff, hog's-hair brush. As a result the picture looked as if it was covered with a sheet of frosted glass : and we were compelled to bring it to a professional restorer to have AE's treatment remedied. Still, the majority of his pictures, painted as they were at one sitting, without niggling or much re-touching, will undoubtedly prove permanent. I have myself several, painted twenty or thirty years ago, which have not altered in the meantime in the slightest degree. The dark-toned ones are more liable, owing to his methods, to deteriorate than those painted with a considerable admixture of flake white.

'Though he will probably always be far more famous as a poet than as a painter, I believe him to have had a streak of genius in the latter capacity. He had a fine sense of colour, a great gift for composition. His draughtsmanship, particularly in figures, left occasionally much to be desired. But, had he painted day in and day out, there can be no doubt that he would have taken rank as one of the most noteworthy painters of his age. The long landscape frieze which he did for Sir Horace Plunkett's house, Kilteragh, at Foxrock, was a composition, well realised, of extraordinary love-

A Memoir of AE

liness. It was certainly AE's masterpiece: and it is a pity of pities that it disappeared in the fire which consumed the house during the Irish Civil War of 1922-23.

'He did a few, a very few, portraits, and was happy in catching a likeness. One of W. B. Yeats as a young man, in chalk, and another of James Stephens, in oils, hung in his own house. As he grew older he seemed to lose his taste for symbolic and mythological subjects and to confine himself mainly to pure landscape. For ten or twelve years before he died he painted little and exhibited not at all.

'In conclusion, it may be interesting to add that in 1910 he told me that the six works of graphic or plastic art which he would most like to possess were these: a certain big landscape by Corot which, from his description, I judged to be the "Souvenir d'Italie"; "A Moorland Scene by Night" by Jean François Millet, which I cannot identify; "Mousehold Heath" by John Crome; "A Sunset" by Rousseau, now in the Lane Collection at the Tate; the statue of Theseus, by Pheidias, and Rembrandt's "Jewish Merchant".'

A Memoir of AE

8

Some of AE's friends regretted the close association with George Moore, which began when Moore came to live in Dublin, and lasted through the ten years of his stay. 'The reader knows', writes Moore in *Hail and Farewell*, ' how impossible it is for me to believe that anyone likes me for my own sake, and, at the end of a week, I was trying to find sufficient reason why AE should seek me out in my garden every afternoon. It could not be the pleasure of my society that attracted him. " He is clearly attracted by something in me that he has been seeking."' The Pharisaic avoidance of Moore in Dublin would have been enough to attract AE to him. But Moore fascinated AE. For one thing, he was the author of what AE always maintained to be one of the greatest of English novels, *The Mummer's Wife*. Perhaps he even divined the essential innocence of Moore's mind, of which an invincible ignorance of the sacrosanct element in life was part, though this seems hardly likely in view of the atrocious characterisation of Moore which he was one day to write in *The Avatars*. Anyhow, throughout Moore's stay, he was Moore's constant companion, and what AE meant to Moore all know who have found delight in Moore's masterpiece. But can we say that AE profited no more from Moore than Socrates may be presumed to have profited from Alcibiades? The gift of himself by an accomplished man of letters, with his wide experience of men and literature, to a little movement which was at the time provincial, was a more effective influence than those who participated in it were inclined to acknowledge, though Moore himself was perhaps over-conscious of its importance. For an estimate of it we have only to ask what, in the eyes at least of the British public, would have been the whole history of the Irish Literary Movement without the genial illumination cast upon it by Moore's narrative. And he gave himself freely, generously, confidingly. His Saturday-night gatherings were a principal feature of AE's life during these ten years; there he practised and perfected himself in his great art of talking. Moore himself was perfect on these occasions—amused, attentive, evocative, appreciative, in his own way as inexhaustible as Russell in reminiscence and invention, often correcting us out of a far wider culture than that with which he was commonly credited. One regrettable result of this intimacy was that AE began to drift somewhat apart from Yeats, who for the carrying on of his dramatic programme had found it expedient to break with Moore.

A Memoir of AE

Yeats had played a great part in Russell's life, both as poet and friend, and now their paths diverged —to meet again, when both were elderly men, in a strangely altered Ireland.

Plunkett, as Vice-President since 1899 of the new Department of Agriculture and Technical Instruction which he had induced the British Government to set up, was now directly exposed to the hostility of the Nationalist party, who accused his Organisation of carrying on ' a cruel war against traders '. In 1906 they captured the Vice-Presidency, and T. W. Russell, succeeding Plunkett, began to cut down and finally withdrew the grants to the Organisation which Plunkett had secured. It was in this phase of its history that AE in 1906 entered on the editorship of the *Irish Homestead*, which he was to hold until its amalgamation with the *Irish Statesman* in 1923, and in accepting it he once more stipulated for his entire freedom. I regret that I have discovered no private correspondence between AE and Plunkett which might throw light on their personal relations. As already suggested, Plunkett was half dreamer, half man born to be king, his function being to support with the sweetness of his approval the subordinates whom he had chosen with royal divination. And as Anderson was his right-hand man, so AE became his spokesman and his Rupert of debate. He had set AE his theme of rural co-operation, and AE's journalism rose like a song out of the bitter newspaper press of Ireland, building up Plunkett's ideal kingdom. People who looked into the *Irish Homestead* to see how AE would write about pigs and poultry shrugged their shoulders when they found perfectly readable discourses, with glints of science, metaphysics and the lore of the East, and hints of AE's peculiar doctrines ; but such people did not realise that the born idealist has an adroitness of his own ; and an economist who combined with a knowledge of the facts of a farmer's life a conviction that the Irish farmer himself was essentially a hero and poet, may have brought a puzzled look into the farmer's face, yet addressed him with an added power. Plunkett, for instance, had aroused a considerable amount of angry comment by his remarks in *Ireland in the New Century*, on the excessive expenditure of Irish money in church-building. AE would never have so imperilled his cause : he would have approached the subject more insidiously and have talked first of the sacred earth we tread, and the soil of Erin holy as Palestine. The *Irish Homestead* may not have been much read by those for whom it was nominally intended ; but the journal became widely known, and AE's name one of note among English and American journalists. A. R. Orage, for instance, a fastidious critic, used to describe Russell's articles as ' the best current writing anywhere ' ; and Mr. Henry Wallace, Secretary of the U.S. Department of Agriculture, relates how eagerly in his youth AE's weekly articles were read aloud in his family. Plunkett grew proud of the little journal, which was a revelation to him of his own idealism, and brought out in him a quasi-royal patronage of poets, though the poets of the Celtic Renascence were not naturally to his taste (through the oaken carvings of his dining-room mantelpiece in Kilteragh ran a line of Kipling). But it was Yeats who had introduced AE, and Plunkett now allowed AE to discover new poet-Organisers. The Plunkett House became a nest of singing-birds, who joined in happy chorus every year in the pages of *The Celtic Christmas*.

In the office with AE sat Susan Mitchell, of the witty tongue, a poetess, whose big brown eyes and mass of red hair had won her a repute for good looks : she suffered cruelly from ill-health, but always maintained a sly cheerfulness, and became the hostess of the office, which throughout the week vied in hospitality to distinguished strangers with AE's home in 17 Rathgar Avenue on Sunday evenings. The pair were a familiar sight in the streets

A Memoir of AE

of Dublin, catching the sardonic eye of Stephen Dedalus as he passed in his now world-famed odyssey. In his tribute to her on her death in March 1926, AE wrote : ' She was of middle-age when I met her, and she became my daily associate in work until she died, but even when she was white-haired she was, I imagine, no older within than when she was the beautiful girl earlier friends than I remember so fondly '. At all times of his life Russell had the faculty, possessed by certain pure-minded men, of attracting to himself the devotion of women, but his biographer must state that in this case his home-life suffered ; though there appeared to be such an understanding between him and his wife that one felt that their domestic affairs were their own concern and no one else's. A Puritan, who rejected from his life all ' romance ', he claimed entire freedom in his friendships with men and women, and it is probable that Mrs. Russell was able to find consolation in the independent exercise of her own social instincts. Along with a vein of genuine poetry in Susan Mitchell there was a turn for humorous verse, which brought out a similar vein in AE, so that the skits which issued from the office were almost indistinguishable as to authorship. George Moore, who froze up at all facetiousness, used to find her witticisms, uttered in her

A Memoir of AE

plaintive contralto voice, rather fatiguing ; and indeed the estrangement which arose ultimately between Moore and Russell had its origin in her book on Moore, a storehouse of all the jokes about him with which her little world of literary Dublin regaled itself. Moore was intensely irritated, suspecting AE to have had a share in it, and he chose to take special offence at some light-hearted comments on his Protestantism.

A visitor to the office, Mrs. McCraith Blakeney, thus records her impressions :

' I went up many broad steps to the well-known big low room that overlooked a wide vista of South Dublin. Susan Mitchell, with her chestnut eyes and frosted chestnut hair, came forward to meet us, and AE rose from his desk with a hasty, hearty gesture and outstretched hand. My first impression was that he was big—shaggy, curiously simple and humble, almost diffident, but unmistakably a source of power. He was not like an Irishman at all ; his dark brown hair grew long and loose, his great russet beard crept up to his broad cheek-bones. His eyes were hidden by his overhanging hair and by big pebble-spectacles, but they twinkled with a large humanity and kindliness that, like his speech, had a northern savour. Two large desks rose like rocks out of a sea of newspapers and literary litter. The walls were covered with brown paper, which was painted with strange figures with many-coloured wings. . . .'

In a letter to Clifford Bax he describes his life:

'If you knew what it meant to write about fifteen columns of journalism every week you would understand after four or five years of it how the thought of writing a line one is not forced to write makes one sick. You would understand me if you could not forgive me. You see, I earn my living in two ways, by agricultural journalism and by painting. I spend five and a half days at the journalism and the other day and a half in painting. If I did not I would go bankrupt. I have a continual headache and am always wondering how long I can go on. . . . I am caught in the wheel and it turns round and round and I with it, and I will be jolly glad when the motion gets too swift and I am shot off into space.' 'I am greatly interested in building up a rural civilisation in Ireland on the lines of the old communes. If you knew what this meant you would be just as interested as I am.'

A Memoir of AE

This busy editor, immersed in controversies, but fond of literary parties in the evenings, ready to talk about everything, reading everything (including detective stories), the intimate of George Moore, might seem a different person from Miss Rea's spiritual mentor, who could ' have no friends outside those who are in terrible earnest ' about life. Even in the Hermetic Society, where he presided every Thursday evening, he seemed glad enough, after a perfunctory lesson in Theosophy, to launch into sociological and political speculation. AE, the ' AEon ', had retreated within himself, only in his private spiritual exercises recovering the memories and impulses recorded still in an occasional poem. But his work was now no drudgery like that at Pim's, and it was with a religious eloquence and persuasiveness that he preached Co-operation, and began to catch glimpses of the solution of all social problems in ' The Co-operative Commonwealth '. An address to the Annual General Meeting of the Irish Agricultural Organisation Society in 1909 on *The Building up of a Rural Civilisation*, published as a pamphlet, was expanded into *Co-operation and Nationality* (1912), a little work which first attracted general attention to AE as a writer on Economics.

In this little treatise he takes full advantage of the

freedom for which he had stipulated in joining Plunkett's movement. He was like a speaker to whom his own supporters listen a little nervously, not knowing to what he will commit them, and indeed Co-operation as AE expounded it grew into a cause associated with the redemption of mankind in a new social order. But if at times he made Plunkett, Anderson and Father Finlay a little uneasy, they probably reminded one another that everyone knew that AE was a poet, and could say things for which, if uttered by themselves, T. W. Russell and John Dillon would have called them to account. A poet, however, no less than a prophet, can get at once to essentials, and there was a refreshing directness in AE's diatribes against those strongholds of Parliamentary nationalism, the Irish country towns:

> 'There are two kinds of towns, the town which exists because it is a centre of production, and the town which exists because it is a centre of distribution.' 'I have prophesied against many Irish country towns for this sin in them, *that they do not produce.*' 'Towns ought to be conductors, catching the lightnings of the human mind, and distributing them all around their area. The Irish country towns only develop mental bogs

about them. We have grown so accustomed to these arid patches of humanity that we accept them in a hopeless kind of way, whereas we should rage and prophesy over them as the prophets of ancient Israel did over Tyre and Sidon. And indeed a lordly magnificence of wickedness is not so hopeless a thing to contemplate as a dead level of petty iniquity, the soul's death in life, without ideas or aspirations.'

AE's remedy was the same as Plunkett's, except that he added the confident vision of an Irish countryside restored to health in rural communes, prefigured in Ireland's ancient history. If rural labour would organise itself into a conscious economic entity to supply without the agency of ' middlemen ' the needs of urban civilisation, there would be constituted a rural better half to urban civilisation, a stable and enduring element in the national life, nearer to nature and to ancestral tradition. Economic independence would generate all the amenities of life, superior amenities, and the seductiveness of the great cities would cease to depopulate the countryside. There would be what had never been in history, a rural civilisation. Instead of the arid country towns there would be thriving villages, or small but ' real ' towns, like

A Memoir of AE

those of ancient Greece or mediaeval Italy, with craftsmen and artists for their citizens. For with economic independence not only would the Irish character mend itself, but from the awakening of the Irish mind would emerge new forms of art and new perceptions of thought.

Rural civilisation ? Does it not seem almost a contradiction in terms ? The country is the country and the town the town, and if you like the country you will hardly wish it civilised. Town and country are magnetic contrasts, necessary to one another. Russell himself, like Socrates and Dr. Johnson, was by nature a townsman : as he confessed to me in the old Theosophic days, ' The full life is in the city '. What seems everywhere in process of happening (regrettably) is the gradual obliteration of any abrupt distinction between town and country. Ireland itself is altering out of all recognition from the Ireland Russell knew forty years ago, and the peasant is vanishing from Ireland as from the whole world. But there was something novel and inspiring in the attention which AE concentrated on the farmer as a human being, and his insistence on filling up the void in the spiritual and intellectual life of the countryside was not without its practical aspect. Agricultural authorities from other lands, attracted to the study of Plunkett's

A Memoir of AE

beneficent movement, were impressed by this earnest voice ; and Mr. H. F. Norman has written of the ' electrical effect his plea for the ideal of the rural community exercised on the hundred and fifty visitors from U.S.A. and Canada in 1913 '.

But to his old friend Weekes, who lived now in London, Russell, as an agricultural organiser and the editor of a small provincial paper, seemed lost to the world. He answers one of Weekes's expostulations :

' My dear boy, a man's success or failure is always with his own soul. You would like to see me well known, writing wise and beautiful books, hailed by the applause of the best critics. I might be all this and a failure in my own eyes, and wretched and unhappy. I am working for causes I feel to be good. I don't care in the least for recognition. In fact I loathe my personal publicity. I can't say that I have lived up to my highest possibilities. Nobody does, but I have not sunk to my worst, and many people do. I will go back to the stars without any flourish of trumpets, but I won't weep as I go back or whine about circumstances. Don't expect anything from me. I am not going anywhere I can be seen.'

A Memoir of AE

9

But Russell himself had begun to believe that a more revolutionary change than the reorganisation of rural life was wanted in society. The years 1911-12 were 'the period of the Great Strikes', during which everyone became aware of some radical social ailment; and AE was no longer the man who had written of his life at Pim's: 'In spite of it all I am not a socialist'. His advocacy of co-operation began to take a turn not altogether acceptable to his colleagues in the I.A.O.S. It was not really the farmer who interested him now, but the farm-labourer, the 'under-dog'. During 1911 he writes to St. John Ervine:

> 'I believe that in a few years we will have broken the back of the middleman in Ireland and the farmers will revert to tillage and dairying, and I hope the labourers will squeeze them as the old landlords did and keep them hard at work. I think a fairly prosperous rural community could exist here if agriculture were syndicalised and the landlord and middleman eliminated and the fields left to the farmers and labourers. I want the labourers to be organised in a trades union, and also to be members of co-operative societies for the purchase of their domestic re-

quirements. . . . I am not so anti-socialistic as might appear from the *Homestead*. I am trying hard to socialise Ireland, only I call it co-operation. If the Home Rule Bill passes I think I can make up a party here which will bring co-operation into the towns and make the artizan his own employer. Ireland is a small country, and it can be done in a generation.'

And about the same time to Clifford Bax:

'I have always been on the side of the outcasts and I hope I always will be. I was moved a couple of days ago to write some doggerel for a little revolutionary sheet in Ireland which appears irregularly when funds can be scraped together to pre-pay a printer who will give no credit:

> Here's a wreath upon their coffins, since no one else is found
> To say a kindly word for my poor brothers in the ground.
> They had no Christian burial when dropt into the sod,
> And they hinted at 'No mercy' who sent them up to God.
> They may have been low rascals, but they showed before they died

A Memoir of AE

> That many-millioned nation which has no soul
> inside
> The fire of the primeval man, a flash of the
> Promethean will,
> Before life's candle fluttered down and Sidney
> Street was still.

I am always shocking my friends by my low tastes, and I am grateful, for it relieves me of their intimacy and the trammels of their respectability. Besides I feel I ought to help you in your fight, to balance the moral effect of another person named Bax, Belfort Bax, who writes the deadliest philosophy I ever came across.'

In Plunkett House and Kilteragh he still conferred with 'respectability'. But his own home in Rathgar Avenue was the meeting-place not only of poets but of agitators, and whosoever had felt the call to foster 'divine discontent' in the underworld.

The publication of his *Collected Poems* (Macmillan, 1913) marked his special place among the poets of his time. The volume included one poem, 'On Behalf of Some Irishmen not Followers of Tradition', which had brought him prominently into public notice, and has probably given him more general fame as a poet than anything else, he wrote:

A Memoir of AE

> We hold the Ireland in the heart
>   More than the land our eyes have seen
> And love the goal for which we start
>   More than the tale of what has been. . . .
> We would no Irish sign efface,
>   But yet our lips would gladlier hail
> The first-born of the Coming Race
>   Than the last splendour of the Gael.
> No blazoned banner we unfold—
>   One charge alone we give to youth,
> Against the sceptred myth to hold
>   The golden heresy of truth.

It is with these words on his lips that AE, as a public figure, should go down to posterity; and it was the impassioned idealist of this poem, with all his powers of invective and direct statement, who now intervened in the stormy Labour disputes in Dublin of 1913.

William Martin Murphy, it will be remembered, had boldly countered Larkin's ' sympathetic strike' with the ' sympathetic lock-out' by four hundred Dublin employers, to whom he had given a lead by refusing to employ in his tram-system anyone who belonged to the Transport Workers' Union. Presently there were 15,000 workless men wandering about the streets, mingled with strange figures out of the underworld. In the blaze of Larkin's agitation the wretchedness of Dublin pauperism was

A Memoir of AE

laid bare to the public view as never before. The English Trade Unions took up the cause of the strikers; the Miners' Federation voted £1000 a week; relief ships with food arrived in the Liffey; and at length Sir George Askwith was directed to hold a Board of Trade enquiry in Dublin Castle. I looked in there one day, and have a vivid recollection of the dark inchoate face of Larkin and of his tall ungainly figure, craning forward as he bellowed forth his arraignment; and opposite him the calm handsome face of Murphy, with trim white beard, speaking just above his breath and glancing occasionally at his angry foe: near him rose from time to time the robust form of his counsel, Thersites Healy, releasing effortlessly his biting speech. Murphy's origins had been as humble as Larkin's, but 'divine discontent' had prompted him to take life in a different spirit; he had built railways and tramways in Africa and England, and now controlled public opinion through the most popular of Irish newspapers, which he owned. The intellectuals were all against him and on Larkin's side, and little he cared: he was indeed one more justification of Bernard Shaw's conception of the Wellingtonian Irishman. After a week, Sir George Askwith issued a statement which was in effect a censure of both Larkin and Murphy; and

A Memoir of AE

Murphy, though the whole British press clamoured against him, and tramless Dublin was weary of walking, repudiated the terms proposed. It was at this point that AE joined in the fray with an 'Open Letter to the Masters of Dublin', printed in the *Irish Times* and circulated as a leaflet. It is a fine example of AE's not infrequent exercises in invective. Murphy, who lived till 1921, was soon to witness the part which the Citizen Army played in the Irish revolution, and perhaps to recognise that there was something more than rhetoric in AE's concluding words:

'You may succeed in your policy [Murphy did succeed] and ensure your own damnation by your victory. The men whose manhood you have broken will loathe you, and will always be brooding and scheming to strike a fresh blow. The children will be taught to curse you, the infant being moulded in the womb will have breathed into its starved body the vitality of hate. It is not they—it is you who are blind Samsons pulling down the social order.'

AE, now prominently associated with Larkin's cause, was invited over to London to speak at a great meeting in the Albert Hall on November 1, to protest against the obstinacy of the employers

A Memoir of AE

and the arrest of Larkin for sedition. Forty thousand people applied for admission, and Bernard Shaw was one of the speakers. It must have been an ordeal for AE, who shrank from public speaking, to rise up before that vast audience, but his speech was received with enthusiasm, and on one subject he spoke with a freedom from which his connection with the I.A.O.S. restrained him in Dublin:

> 'Ah! but I forgot; there has sprung up a third party, who are superhuman beings, they have so little concern for the body at all that they assert it is better for children to be starved than to be moved from the Christian atmosphere of the Dublin slums. Dublin is the most Christian city in these islands. Its tottering tenements are holy. The spiritual atmosphere which pervades them is ample compensation for the diseases which are there and the food which is not there. If any poor parents think otherwise, and would send their children for a little from that earthly paradise, they will find the docks and railway-stations barred by these superhuman beings and by the police, and they are pitched headlong out of the station, set upon and beaten, and their children snatched from them.'

A Memoir of AE

This, of course, is wild language, and AE was to hear a good deal more about it when he returned to Dublin. His courage deserves our admiration, but truth compels me to add that among his many gifts was not the cool instinct of the public man. He was often inclined to use excited language, and then to profess indignant astonishment that he should be taken for anything but a poet and visionary. He defended himself in the London *Times* :

> 'I am charged with being a revolutionary : I who for seven or eight years past have week by week been expounding an orderly evolution of society. I am charged with being against religion : I the sole poet of my generation who has never written a single poem which did not try to express a spiritual mood.'

He was certainly a little exalted at this time. He writes to Yeats, who had also defended Larkin in the *Irish Worker* :

> 'I have a long battle before me and the Church is raging against me all over Ireland, and trying to make my continuance in the Co-operative Movement an impossibility.'

And in a letter to [Sir] J. C. Squire he says :

> 'I came back to find Dublin one prolonged

howl of indignation at my Albert Hall speech. The *Freeman's Journal* leadered my iniquity on Monday, also on Tuesday, also on Wednesday, and only fainted on Thursday through a complete loss of new epithets. The other papers, Unionist and Nationalist, dealt with me good measure pressed down and frothing over. I am now to have a fight for my continuance in the Co-operative Movement. The Committee of the I.A.O.S. at a special meeting on Monday are to consider my sins. The Hibernians have sent round a secret circular to stop the *Homestead*. They know I meant them by my speech about the superhuman. The Church thought I referred to them, and they also had a meeting, hence the I.A.O.S. panic committee to cut me off. It is great fun, but far away from poetry. I daresay the soul will come to my assistance, but what I really want now is a bludgeon, and I could use it too.'

The storm blew over. Plunkett himself had been guilty of indiscretions, and could hardly reprimand Russell, whose services were too important to lose. But Russell did not again offend ; and the interest of Catholic Ireland was bound up with the causes he was henceforth to champion.

A Memoir of AE

10

Though not so far much interested in politics he was of course a Home Ruler, and the I.A.O.S., in common with the rest of Ireland, was awaiting the advent of self-government, now on the Statute Book. The one prosaic fact, viewed with despairing impatience by Irish nationalism and by the poets of the Irish Literary Renascence, was 'the attitude of Ulster'. Yet it cannot be said that the cause of Ulster was wholly distasteful to poets, for in 1912 Kipling published his resounding verses bearing as their title the name of the notorious province. As an Ulsterman, Russell always claimed a special comprehension of the Ulster problem, and he now addressed Kipling in an 'Open Letter', much admired as a piece of invective, in which he contrived to convey in a somewhat unctuous spirit a good deal of insulting suggestion. I did not myself much admire his Letter; and Kipling, after 1916, no doubt felt that events had justified him in including the poem in *The Years Between*.

But now a leader of men, with some of the attributes of Parnell himself, appeared in Ireland, this time among the Unionists of Ulster. Carson has been called a playboy, and certainly when he was on the stage no one else counted; he was able to turn to his own advantage the constantly reiterated accusation of 'bluff' by springing surprises on his opponents; and Parnell himself never provided spectators with better entertainment, if it was only that, than Carson on the night of the gun-running at Larne (24th April, 1914). By this he so won the admiration, expressed in imitation, of the Southern Irish, as to make it now seem a possibility that if unexpected events had not supervened he might have been the leader of more than the Orangemen: as perhaps Redmond may have felt, and later on De Valera, when they fought shy of his proposal for a heart-to-heart talk with them. AE hated everything that Carson stood for, but on reading in MS. St. John Ervine's scornful little book on Carson, he wrote in mild protest:

> 'He is not an attractive personality, this Carson, but he has a kind of power and a character of his own, big in a way in *resistance*, though not in creative statesmanship. He has, like Parnell, the Irishman's faculty of doing the unexpected. When driven into a corner, the unimaginative Irishman will always go outside the convention, and Carson did, and he acted with rather more dignity than Dillon. . . . Sir Horace Plunkett,

A Memoir of AE

who had a good many conversations with him, told me that Carson was the only one of the Ulster leaders who had any sense of responsibility, and the only one who was sympathetic in conversation with Sir Horace's own attempts at a solution of the Ulster trouble. So I oppose these facts to your scornful dismissal of him altogether as the last stage Irishman.'

But of the various quasi-military organisations in Ireland in this year, probably Larkin's and Connolly's Citizen Army had most of his sympathy, Captain J. R. White, the soldier of 'divine discontent', being one of his intimates. In another letter to Ervine he writes :

'I am sure your socialism is all right for England. If I were living there I would be a socialist or else an anarchist, something devilishly extreme anyhow, not in the hopes of doing anything, but of keeping my own soul alive.'

Luckily for him he could keep his soul alive in the work of the I.A.O.S., and Plunkett's influence, now as always, exercised a restraint upon him.

A Memoir of AE

11

But the Great War broke out, and a hush fell for a time over the threat of strife in Ireland.

In one of his letters to Yeats, AE recalls a prophecy of 'H.P.B.' that 'by 1914 there would be a squaring of accounts between races'. 'I remembered this prophecy when the War broke out, and I think her statement that these two countries [France and England] would very soon fall into their Iron Age is true. I think Ireland will lift itself out of its long obscuration by virtue of an idealism which is in its people.' When it became clear that the War was to be a long one, the mood of Ireland, even while it was still spoken of as the 'one bright spot', began to change, and it bethought itself of its old maxim, 'England's difficulty, Ireland's opportunity'. In a letter to Charles Weekes of October 1914, AE expresses his forebodings:

'You asked in your letter, why was I scared about Ireland. I can hardly tell you, because I can hardly explain it to myself. I have a conviction deep within me that we are going to have one more heart-searching trial, baring our lives to the very spirit, and that within the next few

A Memoir of AE

years. Maybe much sooner. The dragons of the past have not died and were only sleeping, and recent events have stirred them, both the events in Ireland and the European War. I may be mistaken. The best thing which could happen to us would be a foray of about 2000 Germans in the north and a rush of the rest of Ireland to rescue Ulster. But the gods do not arrange things as in the story-books.'

'War', he writes in *The National Being*, 'brings about an eruption of the arcane and elemental forces which lie normally in the pit of human life, as the forces which cause earthquakes lie normally asleep in the womb of the world.' These arcane forces are the theme of the remarkable series of poems which he contributed to the London *Times*, afterwards collected in a booklet, *Gods of War* (1915). They certainly were not songs with which a warrior would advance with new courage into the fight, but fierce denunciations of the guilt of the nations concerned and apocalyptic warnings of wrath to come. They strike one now, perhaps, as a little strained and inhuman. They were written by no particular friend to the cause of the Allies; and what the moment called for was less a denunciation of warfare than some enlightenment on the ethical question. Indeed, the true Arjuna at this moment was the thoughtful portion of the British public, which was divided on the question ; and the answer of AE was not that of Krishna. When, a few years later, the question arose of the right of Ireland to assert in arms its independence of England, he took a different tone. But the British public was in the mood for solemn thought, and AE never attained more impressive poetic eloquence than in these poems.

' I am growing excited about the War ', he writes to Weekes, 'because when it ends I think we are bound to have social revolution all over Europe.' Yet though he was ' above the combat ', and would have liked Ireland to be so too, he could write thus feelingly to the same friend :

' One lives with a strained heart all the time. I have so many friends in this struggle. Two dear boys, sons of Anderson, both were killed, one a week ago, and the other a few weeks before that. I knew them since they were children. Other friends of mine are out on land and sea, some mine-sweeping, some on the battle-ships, some in the trenches, while some are missing, all friends of our Movement here, people who were about me often and the best kind of Irish. Our

A Memoir of AE

civilisation really does beget fine people with bodies, sheaths for the unrusted steel of the spirit. There are many I knew, and hardly expected that so flashing a spirit would be drawn from the sheath of the body when there was need.'

Nationalism in Ireland is a perfectly natural and genuine sentiment, but unfortunately it does not cover the facts in modern Ireland : the identity of civilisation on both sides of the Irish Sea has also to be taken into account, militant nationalism being only really justified when its cause is that of free human development. It was possible to be a good Irishman and yet not to feel in oneself a much greater difference from an Englishman than an Englishman of Lancashire feels from one of Devon. Such Irishmen had come to be called by what was meant to be the opprobrious name of 'West Briton', but they might retort that Irish nationalism itself had something in common with provincialism. With the attempted revival of the Irish language, however, a new party had risen which claimed that there were two civilisations, the Irish and the English. Russell was not a Sinn Féiner, but his little work, *The National Being* (1916), is an attempt to reconcile his ideal of the Co-operative Commonwealth with the belief in a distinct Irish civilisation. It is one of his best-known works, and as he writes to Prof. J. M. Gaus of Wisconsin,

> 'it has been translated into a number of European languages, and has also been reprinted in India and I think translated there, as Tagore wished Indians to study it.'

And in a letter to Miss Willy Denijs, he says :

> 'The civil conscription idea was put into operation in Bulgaria. A friend of mine gave the book to a Bulgarian statesman ; and after the War, as they were not allowed to have an army, the minister thought of my idea and put it into operation. There was a Report on the subject issued by the Labour Branch of the League of Nations after the scheme was in operation two years. I do not know whether it is still working, as the minister who brought it in was assassinated. I hope not because he applied my idea.' [1]

Writing on a subject which he has made his own, AE makes the Co-operative Commonwealth seem reasonable and attractive ; but the notion of

---

[1] I have not been able to verify the statements in these letters.

A Memoir of AE

a flame of national consciousness lit from a divine origin in the Celtic past is the fable of a poet. Such a theory of nationality is particularly hard to apply to the history of Ireland, where, if an Irishman like Russell himself, without a drop of Celtic blood, could claim to belong to it, the English in Ireland, with their seven hundred years of 'interference', have some reason to resent their sentence of excommunication. He would have replied, however, that the 'national will', which is never wrong, had never consented to the direction of English ideas, and he would doubtless have quoted a favourite passage to this effect from John Mitchel's *History*. This is indeed the strong point in the Irish claim to separate nationality, and it was owing to the persistence of this refusal to our own day that English statesmen finally threw up their hands in despair.

The occasion of *The National Being* was 'the birth of the infant State of Ireland', in other words, the passing of the Home Rule Bill—'a poor, miserable thing', as he called it privately, 'as bad as it can be—but when this Home Rule question is swept out of the way, we shall get a new sort of nationality, and this is what we are building up'. How had AE come to believe, in his own language, that 'the mighty labour of nation-building' was 'at once

A Memoir of AE

the noblest and most practicable of all enterprises'? Was this the task for which he himself was really fitted, and which he could do best? It must be remembered that, unworldly as he was, he had his full share of the ambitious energy of the North of Ireland race to which he belonged, and he had been fired by the great example of Alexander Hamilton, whose Life by F. S. Oliver was a frequent text of his discourse. Might not he himself be the Alexander Hamilton of the Irish Co-operative Commonwealth? Yet ably though he argued for the economic advantages of co-operation, it was of the spiritual change to be effected through it that he chiefly thought. 'The co-operative organisations now being formed in Ireland and all over the world will, I am certain, persist, and grow into vaster things than we dream of; but the really important change they will bring about in the minds of men will be psychological. . . . The Co-operative Movement is a vast turning movement of humanity heavenwards, or at least to bring them face round to the Delectable City.' But even as he worked at *The National Being,* the decline of interest in the Co-operative ideal—in England owing to the War, and in Ireland, to the growing clamancy of the Sinn Féin movement—was a disappointment to him; and the interest of readers in his book has been due, perhaps chiefly, to its exposition of a mystical nationalism.

A lady—Mrs. McCraith Blakeney—records a visit to the office in The Plunkett House a few weeks before the Rising of 1916. 'I said to Susan Mitchell as we left him, "Does he know how great his influence is?" "But is it?" she said sadly. "But he *is* great!" "Not in Ireland to-day," she murmured, with a sad little waft of vision.'

12

Yet now and still for many years AE was looked upon as a kind of 'key-personality' for his country's problems, and a visit to Ireland was not complete without an interview with him. Probably there are men nearly everywhere, talkers and philosophers, who loom larger to their little circle than the great ones of the world outside. But there was nothing merely local or provincial in AE, and what strangers commonly said of him was that they had never met anyone like him. His mind rose as free from its surroundings as Coleridge's, and strangers at his Sunday evening gatherings exceeded in their eulogies the friends who took AE for granted, and perhaps hardly realised their dependence on him.

A Memoir of AE

There was no important intellectual or social movement on which he had not some authoritative comment, no important book with which he had not somehow made himself acquainted. His radiant presence diffused happiness and confidence. Novelists, coveting so rare a character, put him into their stories, and George Moore, in his famous Trilogy, took credit for having spread the almost incredible legend of AE. It was said of him that he lived in an atmosphere of adoration, but this was not the impression of strangers. Here for instance is a newspaper cutting, of uncertain date, one of many similar testimonies:

'I have only once seen and heard AE. That was when he was in London, a while ago, one of several speakers at a public meeting discussing the social and economic condition of Ireland, and, when his turn came, he spoke with much evident depth of feeling, so simply and with such clear sincerity, that, for me, he made all the other speakers seem slight and ineffective; and it pleases me to find that impression confirmed by Mr. Cumberland, who writes of a Dublin visit: "On the evening of the following day I was taken to see George Russell, far and away the greatest Irishman of the present generation. Poet, painter, politician, mystic, editor, man of business, organiser, his life is full to overflowing. So great is his genius for friendship that men of directly opposite political beliefs find in him their ideal man." He goes on to describe the group of others in the room —men, he says, who tried to be clever; and " for some time this big bearded man, with his great shoulders and face in which there is no guile, remained silent and ruminative, only occasionally interrupting to state in simple quiet words laws so wise that in a moment they annihilated the brilliant twaddle. I sat apart, waiting for Russell's voice, watching his every movement, trying in vain to capture his secret. All I saw was a kindly, humorous, wise man, of enormous tact and great toleration. If vanity is the womb of genius, then Russell has no genius. He is simple, he is courteous, he is free from pose, best of all, he does not talk cleverly. When at midnight I left, he accompanied me to the hall-door, and I could not but feel as he took my hand that I had for some few hours been in the presence of a man of noble mind and strange, disturbing genius."'

Some comparison between Yeats and Russell— the *Dichterpaar* of modern Irish literature—may

A Memoir of AE

be expected; and the first thing to be remarked is that it was the man of much rarer poetic endowment and wider mundane experience whose interests were the more restricted and specialised. The field of action with Yeats—the trained, reserved and secretive literary artist—was mainly the affairs of the Abbey Theatre; while Russell's mind expatiated in political, economic and even cosmical problems. Yeats, as a public man, rose to his height in the uproar over Synge's *Playboy*; while Russell, on various exciting occasions—the strike of 1913, the question of conscription in Ireland during the Great War, the Convention of 1917, the death by self-starvation of Terence MacSwiney, and other tragic happenings—drew universal attention to his indignant figure. Yet the truth of Goethe's maxim, ' In der Beschränkung zeigt sich erst der Meister', was never better illustrated than here, and Yeats remained the master-spirit, his fine workmanship and objectivity being altogether beyond Russell's rivalry; and in character and disposition the two were almost antipathetic. Even as a public man Russell hardly ranked with Yeats, who has a real talent for public appearances. Yet Russell, as an embodiment of the beliefs and principles of the Irish Literary Movement, was to it a tower of strength, and

A Memoir of AE

without him it would not have maintained its air of transcendental illumination, or even its transcendental nationalism. Yeats, like a Parnell of literature, held aloof for the most part from the younger recruits to his movement, an attitude favourable to the authority of Irish literature's unquestioned chief: though indeed, when he liked to do so, no one could give more helpful or discriminating advice to a young poet than Yeats. But nothing delighted Russell so much as the discovery of new talent, and when any youthful poet presented himself, the big man would rise up and embrace him like a father.

Thus the younger poets—Padraic Colum, Seumas O'Sullivan, James Stephens and others—gathered round AE rather than Yeats, of whom they saw little. The actual father of the literary movement, Standish O'Grady, who was not particularly satisfied with his offspring, kept mostly to himself, wandering about the country on his bicycle. An interesting friendship which AE had made earlier in the century should be mentioned. One day, in the National Gallery, he engaged in conversation with a visitor, whom, from his leisurely air and large comfortable suit, he took to be most likely an Indian Civil Servant. AE talked with his usual eloquence, and seemed, as the visitor

A Memoir of AE

afterwards said, to 'know a devil of a lot about pictures'. 'The present writer once talked for an hour with Bernard Shaw', AE writes in the *Irish Statesman*, 'and had not the faintest notion that it was that famous man, whose features were so familiar in portraits, who was speaking to him, although thinking back over the conversation every sentence uttered bore the stamp of an intellectual mint which was familiar.' They parted without learning each other's name: but that evening, at the Abbey Theatre, AE recognised his new acquaintance in the stalls in front of him, and after the performance he and Bernard Shaw were introduced to one another. Shaw was a frequent visitor at Kilteragh, and the two became good friends; and they spoke from the same platform, as already mentioned, in the Albert Hall.

Some mention should be made of an early friend of Russell, Philip Francis Little, who led the uncompanioned life of the crazy; though in talking to him and looking into his radiant, sardonic face, one felt that the reputation of being mad may have suited him as well as it suited Hamlet. Readers of Oliver Gogarty's *As I was going down Sackville Street* will remember that amid his wild poems occur lines of extreme beauty. AE, in one of his lectures delivered in the United States, on 'Some Characters of the Irish Literary Movement ', gives this account of Little :

> ' Philip Little, of all people I knew, had brought about the most complete harmony between his inner and his outer life. He was inspired by Catholic mysticism, and I fancy his family, though sincere in their piety, were taken aback by the realism of his acceptance of the instruction he received. Once the boy went out in a new suit of clothes. He came back dressed in rags. He had met a beggar and had exchanged clothes with him, for he thought that the beggar needed the warm clothes more than he did. We became great friends, and after a little he said to me very affectionately : " There is an over-turned railway-truck on the East Pier of Kingstown. We two shall live there and we shall teach the people, and we shall be known as The Wanderers. The people may jeer at us, but they will get tired of jeering at us sooner than we will get tired of doing good to them." I tried to suppress a smile and be as solemn as Philip, but he saw the slight curl about my lips and pointed a finger at me : " You smile," he said, " you never saw me smile." Herein he did himself an injustice, for he had a rich sense of humour. . . . He once asked me to

visit him. I found him isolated in the house of his family, and he thought it necessary to explain to me why none of them were present. "I am very fond of my people," he said, "but they cannot get on with me. Whenever I think of anything, something says to me 'You think so. Why don't you say so? You are a coward,' and I say, 'I am damned if I am,' and out it comes, and just because of that my people are paying me one hundred and fifty a year to live away from them." Then his humour broke out. "I think it should be two hundred, don't you?"

'His conversation had often the romantic eloquence of his verse, and I would try to recall phrases after I left him. Once when he was speaking of Hannibal, he said: "When Hannibal came near Rome, Rome shook as the palm-tree when the lion rubs against it". He seemed to me like one who should have been driving the huge mastodons of thought, but had come to a world dwindled in size, and he had to talk to little people who shrank from him, and left him in a solitude where he became more remote from them, and at last spoke a language they could not understand.'

The 'over-turned truck' was the occasion of a literary squabble. Russell was fond of telling the

A Memoir of AE

story, and was helping George Moore to turn it into a play, when Yeats suddenly discomfited both of them by publishing his play, based on the same subject, *Where there is Nothing*, as a supplement in Griffith's paper *The United Irishman*. Moore now declared that he felt towards Yeats ' exactly as if he had stolen my spoons '; and Yeats was henceforth to maintain towards Moore that air of amused hostility into which his early acclaim of ' the Irish Aristophanes ' finally dwindled.

Since Moore had gone to live in London in 1911 he had seen little of AE, and passing through Dublin towards the end of the War, he professed to find a great change in his former hero:

' I was amused and saddened ', he wrote to me, ' by Russell's show of omniscience. It took a long time to turn his head, but I'm afraid he has donned the prophet's mantle and will never shake himself free again. The eye-glass of " vision " dangles from his button-hole [and is] too much in evidence. He is without the essential humour.'

Moore had never got over his suspicions about Susan Mitchell's book, and was fond of saying that in the Pandora-box of AE's attributes an imp of malice had been left at the bottom—an imputation

A Memoir of AE

which AE's admirers will think hardly worth recording. Yet mingled with all AE's radiant kindliness was a detached observation of his friends' foibles, which was part of his own enormous self-confidence. As I am indulging in indiscreet quotation, it will not, I hope, do worse than amuse Yeats if I quote the following analysis of his character by his old friend, in a letter which Moore sent on to Gosse as 'too good to be lost'. A copy in Gosse's hand was found among the latter's papers, and Mr. Philip Gosse kindly enables me to give the letter here:

> 'Your account of Yeats is very amusing, quite in the *Ave Vale* mood, but I don't think you have dealt yet seriously with the psychology of Yeats. He began about the time of *The Wind among the Reeds* to do two things consciously, one to create a "style" in literature, the second to create or rather to re-create W. B. Yeats in a style which would harmonise with the literary style. People call this posing. It is really putting on a mask, like his actors, Greek or Japanese, a mask over life. The actor must talk to the emotion on the mask, which is a fixed emotion. W. B. Y. began twenty years ago vigorously defending Wilde against the charge of being a poseur. He said it

was merely living artistically, and it was the duty of everybody to have a conception of themselves, and he intended to conceive of himself. The present W. B. Y. is the result. The error in his psychology is, that life creates the form, but he seems to think that the form creates life. If you have a style, he argued once with me, you will have something to say. He seems to have also thought, though he never said so, that if you make a picturesque or majestic personality of yourself in appearance, you will become as wonderful inside as outside. He has created the mask and he finds himself obliged to speak in harmony with the fixed expression of the mask, and that accounts for the lifelessness of his later talk and writing. His memories of his childhood are the most vacant things man ever wrote, pure externalities, well written in a dead kind of way, but quite dull except for the odd flashes. The boy in the book might have become a grocer as well as a poet. Nobody could be astonished if this had been issued as a novel, part one, to find in part two the hero had for some reason given up thinking of literature and become a merchant. Why does he do it? We are interested in Yeats's inner mind, whatever it is, but not in anecdotes of things he saw and whose effect on his own mood is not clear. He bores me terribly now, and he was once so interesting. You are a humorist and a novelist, and he is subject to your art. I want life and thought, and he talks solemn platitudes under the impression that this nonsense is arcane wisdom. Any bit of pedantry a couple of hundred years old seems to him to have a kind of divine authority. But in a way we are interested in him still because of his past. We go to hear him as we go to see the tomb of Shakespeare or the Italian garden where Keats lies. The only difference is that Yeats is his own coffin and memorial tablet. Why can't he be natural? Such a delightful creature he was when young! And at rare moments when he forgets himself he is still interesting as ever almost.'

Yeats and AE were destined to become good friends again and fellow-workers in Dublin. Of Moore, however, though he and AE continued to maintain a show of friendliness, AE's real judgment is probably conveyed in the passage of *The Avatars*, to be mentioned later, in which he seems to relieve himself of long-accumulated feelings of inner antagonism.

13

Even AE required a holiday, and in the early summer every year he packed up his painting materials and set off for Donegal. At the back of Marble Hill, the beautifully situated home of Mr. and Mrs. Hugh Law, looking out on Sheep Haven, there is a white-washed cottage which might serve as the best visible memorial of AE, for it was here, as he said at the end of his life, that he had spent his happiest days. The 'cottage-studio', as Mr. Law kindly reminds me, ' consists of one large room and a half-loft, over the rail of which hangs a piece of stuff embroidered for AE by Mrs. Law with a design of fishes and waves. On the great stone above the hearth is the " sword of light " painted by himself.' AE was one of those who need at least ' one friend to whom to whisper, Solitude is sweet '. He had quite thrown off the diffidence which had once kept him dumb in uncongenial company, and took the lead accorded him in conversation, or even in games and excursions ; and as he worked at his pictures, generally completing two each day from twilight sketches he had made overnight, he would talk uninterruptedly with anyone who sat with him ; occasionally issuing forth to commune with the almost unearthly

A Memoir of AE

beauty of that broken coast, with its rocky inlets and silvery beaches. He came to think of this corner of Donegal as his own peculiar spiritual kingdom, and it supplied the themes of his pictures and many of his poems; and in his last days at Bournemouth he was still full of the hope that he would return to end his days there.

Except for the visit to Donegal, he seldom allowed himself a holiday, but occasionally the attraction of good company was too strong to resist. Professor Bodkin has this note of a week-end at Virginia, Co. Cavan, in September 1914, with AE and James Stephens:

> 'We had a wonderful week-end there. AE painted in Lord Headfort's woods amid thousands of pheasants, till we were all ejected by a keeper. We rowed on the lake, where in brilliant sunshine James Stephens composed and recited to us his poem, "Washed in silver is the moon". In the evenings we capped verses, and when our stock of quotations was exhausted, I went to the village and bought a pack of cards and a large bag of pink comfits for use as counters, and taught the two poets to play poker. AE proved a master of the game and rooked us both. On the journey back to Dublin he produced the

THE "COTTAGE-STUDIO" AT MARBLE HILL

AE ON THE SANDS BELOW MARBLE HILL

comfits and the cards, made a table with our suit-cases, had the door of the railway carriage locked, and played with equal efficiency all the way up to town. I don't think he ever played the game again, and he used to get a little disconcerted whenever I alluded to the escapade in the company of his more serious followers.'

The ancient fern-covered oaks in the woods at Raheen, Co. Clare—' said to be one of the few remaining parts of the primeval forest of Ireland '—are the subject of many of his later pictures. Here lives Edward MacLysaght, poet and agricultural organiser, and at Easter 1916 AE was his guest. On the Tuesday morning they set off to the railway station, 24 miles distant, to catch the train for Dublin, 'without any idea that anything at all serious had happened there '. Mr. MacLysaght continues :

'We caught the train at Nenagh, and at Cloughjordan it began to be obvious that something was amiss. . . . At Ballybrophy we found we could get no further. We began to hear rumours, news even. The Sinn Féiners had Dublin taken, had every position of importance in their possession. I was beginning to feel a sadness mixed with a kind of elation; I saw nothing but half-incredulous amusement on people's faces and in their remarks. AE said something he had heard from Nathan or John MacNeill; it was taken up by listeners eager for gossip, whence all news was derived, and became a rumour before we left the station. We turned back to Raheen and spent the day in discussing a situation we knew nothing about.

'Next morning we set off for Limerick: everywhere we had to produce our licences and identify ourselves to plain-clothes policemen. AE was raging that he had not gone by the early train. I had a longing to be at the centre of things, but I let him voyage off by a train on an adventurous attempt to get home to Dublin by himself.

'Well, Russell told me afterwards that he got to Ballybrophy without incident, but that the remainder of the journey was very difficult. He drove part of it, and walked 14 miles, but was not fired at or molested by any armed forces. I believe he arrived at 17 Rathgar Avenue the next morning, but unfortunately I cannot clearly remember did he spend the night out, or just how long he took to cover the 120 miles from Limerick.'

I lived not far from AE, further out towards the country, and he used to come out to me during those awful days of a glorious spring, while all work was held up, and the air throbbed with machine-guns, sniping and explosions. Then came a lull, and presently the appalling announcements of the executions. Even if Ireland had been in the charge of men with a native understanding of Ireland, they would have had to weigh the problem whether the leaders of the Rising would be a greater danger as convicts or martyrs; yet it is hard to believe that they could have repeated the mistake of their ancestors with Emmet, or, washing their hands of responsibility, like Pilate and Asquith, have handed over the culprits to the soldiers. One thing is certain, that Pearse would have chosen martyrdom; and as he faced the firing-squad in the prison-yard he must have felt that he had done what he had wanted to do.

To Russell the Rising was a sequel to the Labour troubles of 1913. He writes to Charles Weekes (May 1916):

'Nobody, Unionist or Nationalist, agrees with my opinions. Personally, I believe there would have been no revolt if the employers and authorities had not been so unmerciful and unjust during the Great Strike. They left Labour inflamed. I wrote then a letter suppressed

A Memoir of AE

here but which appeared in *The Times*, in which I said, if the authorities were wanting to make Dublin a place with the bombs blazing in the street they were going the right way about it. It was Labour supplied the passional element in the revolt. It had a real grievance. The cultural element, poets, Gaels, etc., never stir more than one per cent of a country. It is only when an immense injustice stirs the workers that they unite their grievances with all other grievances. The stirring element in this was Labour. Connolly was the strong man and intellect in the Rising, and he, I believe, was jeering at the Sinn Féiners as people who talked and did nothing for many months. But our politicians all want to make party capital out of the trouble, and they hate Labour questions being discussed as they are all equally inhuman in regard to them.'

A few days later, when Weekes had urged him to give a lead to public opinion:

'If any honest man expressed his views on the Irish Revolt with absolute lucidity and fearlessness, whether he was Unionist or Nationalist, he would find, first, that no paper would have the courage to print what he wrote, and secondly, if it was printed he would find himself in jail. I asked my own soul about all this trouble and got, not opinions, but a direction of feeling, and what I wrote under that inspiration I do not intend to make public, simply because I am in a movement which is non-political, and I am an important person in it, and any statement made by me might create a split, and cause intense anger in a movement hitherto free from political passions, and in my opinion the only hope of Ireland. . . .'

The allusion may be to his verses, *Salutation*, printed for private circulation in the following year. As they do not appear in his *Collected Poems*, they may be given here :

> Their dream had left me numb and cold,
> But yet my spirit rose in pride,
> Refashioning in burnished gold
> The images of those who died
> Or were shut in the penal cell.
> Here's to you, Pearse, your dream not mine,
> But yet the thought for this you fell
> Has turned life's waters into wine.
>
> I listened to high talk from you,
> Thomas MacDonagh, and it seemed
> The words were idle, but they grew
> To nobleness by death redeemed.

A Memoir of AE

Life cannot utter words more great
Than life can meet with sacrifice.
High words were equalled by high fate.
You paid the price, you paid the price.

The hope lives on age after age
Earth in its beauty might be won
For labour as a heritage.
For this has Ireland lost a son.
This hope into a flame to fan
Men have put life by with a smile.
Here's to you, Connolly, my man,
Who cast the last torch on the pile.

Here's to the women of our blood
Stood by them in the fiery hour,
Rapt lest some weakness in their mood
Rob manhood of a single power.
You, brave on such a hope forlorn,
Who smiled through crack of shot and shell,
Though the world cry on you with scorn,
Here's to you, Constance, in your cell.

Here's to you, men I never met,
Yet hope to meet behind the veil
Thronged on some starry parapet
That looks down upon Inisfail,
And see the confluence of dreams
That clashed together in our night,
One river born from many streams,
Roll in one blaze of blinding light.

A Memoir of AE

In the years that followed, 'Ireland', writes Russell, 'was veritably the country of the young. Youth dominated the political life of Ireland. Its elders shivered, half fascinated, half terrified by the exploits of youth. There were terrible as well as noble things done.' Whatever the reason, the light of AE's name shone most clearly on the other side of the Irish Sea, and while it was from him that foreign visitors continued to seek illumination on the dark problems of Ireland, his influence counted for little in the councils of Sinn Féin. Just before the Insurrection, Griffith had attacked him bitterly in his paper *Nationality*. But among those who frequented his house in Rathgar Avenue on Sunday evenings were many about whom the police were curious, and it was probably watched, for one evening Madame Gonne and an English M.P., Joe King, were arrested as they left it. At Whitsuntide in 1917 there was a round-up of Sinn Féiners, and Russell writes excitedly to Sir William Rothenstein:

'The devils are let loose in Ireland, also some deities. The stop-press out a few minutes ago announces a general strike of all Irish workers as a protest against the infamous treatment of Irish political prisoners who are taken from their families, imprisoned and not tried. Most of them are innocent of any crime except that of loving their country. Where it will end, God alone knows. I think the gang in power want to provoke a rising that they may have another Amritsar here. It is difficult to keep cool.'

14

During 1917, AE again came into great prominence in Ireland through his advocacy of Dominion Home Rule. Sir Horace Plunkett had been moving restlessly between Dublin and London, plotting conciliation, and it was probably in the Plunkett House that the idea of an Assembly of Notables, representing the various conflicting interests of Irish life, originated. AE set to work and contributed to the *Irish Times* a series of articles, entitled *Thoughts for a Convention* : they were reprinted as a pamphlet, and were widely influential in preparing the minds of Unionists for some drastic change in the framework of Irish government.

'I am told my articles have had an immense effect', he writes to Weekes. 'The editor told me that I had shaken the Unionist faith to its innermost tabernacle. It seemed to me that I was writing obvious things, but I do not know

A Memoir of AE

what the Government intend to do about the Convention. If it is well done, and really representative of Irish brains, I think it might settle the Anglo-Irish question. It requires a good Chairman, a real difficulty. . . .'

General Smuts, who was approached, declined to serve; also the Chief Secretary, Mr. Duke; finally Sir Horace Plunkett was the inevitable choice. Sinn Féin was withheld by its principles from attendance, so that the Convention was really like a Homeric intervention of elders in the quarrel of two angry antagonists, Sinn Féin and ' Ulster ', of whom one refused to be present, while the other threatened at any moment to walk out of the court. AE's writings had marked him out for a prominent part in the deliberations, and he and MacLysaght were of special importance as being the nearest approach to representatives of Sinn Féin in the assembly, though they entered it under the stigma (from the point of view of Sinn Féin) of nomination by the government. It thus fell to AE to be the principal spokesman in opposition to ' Ulster '. At certain moments he was the central figure in the assembly; and seasoned politicians, fastidious scholars, ecclesiastical dignitaries and industrial magnates, all attended closely to the bearded artist-

A Memoir of AE

prophet, with his unabashed spiritual idealism, as he brought out his facts and figures. As various members of the Convention still say,[1] none of the speakers left a deeper impress on the deliberations. It would be hard to decide whether the attitude of 'Ulster', in attending the Convention without any intention of changing its mind, was less reasonable than that of Sinn Féin, which refused to attend it at all. Anyhow, the absence of Sinn Féin threw AE into the somewhat invidious position of direct antagonism to 'Ulster'. The argument turned chiefly on the proposed fiscal arrangements between Great Britain and Ireland, on the details of which AE exhibited a mastery which earned him the respect of his opponents. But when it became clear that 'Ulster' could not be induced by argument to do what the Convention had no power of forcing it to do, Russell and Mr. MacLysaght decided on the gesture of withdrawal.[2]

[1] Mr. Stephen Gwynn, for instance, who also writes: 'I find that Lord Londonderry was much impressed by AE, and said his scheme was the only workable one put forward'.

[2] The late Mr. H. M. Pollock, however, the principal spokesman of the Ulster Unionists, in reply to an enquiry on this subject, wrote: 'Russell did not withdraw from the Irish Convention because of his disagreement with the Ulster delegates, but rather because of the disputes which constantly occurred amongst the Southern representatives'.

A Memoir of AE

This action of Russell's was a great blow to Sir Horace Plunkett, who said privately that he would have been angry with anyone but Russell. Had Plunkett reason to feel aggrieved? Or could AE be accused of any disloyalty? No doubt, in entering the Convention, he had stipulated on his entire freedom, and any regret he felt on leaving it was on Plunkett's account. Probably Plunkett alone impersonated the hope expressed by the Prime Minister in his 'Letter of Invitation': 'Would it be too much to hope that Irishmen of all creeds and parties might meet together for the purpose of drafting a constitution for their country?' 'Poor Plunkett!' AE was one day to call him. He was certainly the most attractive figure of his time in Irish public life, the only one whom it was 'good to think of'. Yet it is hard to think of any statesman whose best efforts on behalf of his country have been received with colder or more mocking ingratitude.

Shortly after Russell's withdrawal from the Convention he writes to Mr. Cecil Harmsworth:

> 'I retired from the Convention because I could do no more there. I knew what would settle the Irish question and be accepted by Sinn Féiners as well as by Nationalists, and what

Unionists have always said privately and sometimes publicly would be the only settlement. But the Ulster people have tied their souls into knots and won't have anything. . . . It is not the Irish people who are hindering a settlement, but the pledges to the people of Belfast, nothing else. . . . My belief is that it is dangerous to the Empire to give self-government to Ireland unless it is the kind of government which will satisfy the Irish people, and nothing less than fiscal autonomy will satisfy them. . . . I have the worst forebodings about Ireland in the future.'

Russell made many friends at the Convention, and was regarded by many outside Ireland as its principal interpreter to the outside world. It was in this character that he protested against the proposed extension of Conscription to Ireland in a vehement letter to the *Manchester Guardian*, reprinted as a pamphlet, *Conscription in Ireland: a Warning to England*. On the very day on which the Report of the Convention was handed in, the British authorities announced their intention, and the response in Ireland was a revelation of how completely they had been misinformed about Ireland by their trusted advisers. To Russell himself, the

A Memoir of AE

essential Ireland was still the Chosen People of his beautiful poem 'Michael', composed about this time—

> The army of the Gaelic mind,
> Still holding through the Iron Age
> The spiritual heritage,

and he was only withheld from casting in his lot with Sinn Féin by his belief in the economic interdependence of the two islands, as well as by his horror of physical violence. He was therefore really of little account in an Ireland which now began to make up its mind that if it were compelled to fight, it would fight England.

15

The essential Ireland, after all, was Catholic Ireland, from which Russell was excluded, as may be judged from the numerous passages in his letters in which he speaks of his real function in Ireland as being that of a 'disseminator of heresies': these heresies being, however, the original beliefs of Ireland's 'ancestral self'. He writes to St. John Ervine:

'I am taking no thought or rather part in Irish politics. I feel like a man watching an

A Memoir of AE

avalanche sliding down a hill who knows that nothing can stay it, and action is useless until the avalanche rests. I dread the application of Conscription here because one million people are pledged to resist its application by every means in their power and there is bound to be bloodshed, and I am convinced if French forces it as he threatens after October, that it will mean inextinguishable hatred for all things British in Ireland for generations. Sir Horace, always an optimist, is trying to bring about some movement of moderate men in an immoderate country. I doubt his success with the present régime. I don't myself want to intervene further. The Convention gave me enough politics to last my lifetime, and I will now try to breed heresies which interest me more. Macmillan & Co. are bringing out a book of mine this year I think, which will finally make it impossible for me to take part in politics in Ireland, as it is full of religious heresies and will give me a bad name. But I have had that often and can stand it.'

Anyone who has read *The Candle of Vision*, the book here alluded to, may be inclined to smile at Russell's anticipation that in the midst of Ireland's

A Memoir of AE

political preoccupation the book would excite alarm and animosity against him, and it may even seem to invalidate his claim to an intimate knowledge of Ireland that he should have thought Ireland ripe for heresy. But he would hardly have felt so much interest in Irish politics had he not believed that the political ferment, associated with the Gaelic Revival, was the reawakening of an ancient spirit long overlaid by an exotic pietism. AE has left so gentle a memory that it may seem invidious to suggest that his desire to distinguish himself as a heretic indicates a certain perversity in his mind. 'I go one better than the Gospels,' he writes to Weekes, 'I pray not merely for my enemies but to have enemies to keep me alive.' But *The Candle of Vision* was not a book to make enemies; and as regards heresy, it was only in relation to Theosophy that AE might perhaps be called a heretic; for in withdrawing, in 1898, from membership of the Theosophical Society he had claimed his freedom, and since then in the Hermetic Society had been instructing the small group of his disciples in a system of beliefs in which Ireland resumed its ancient character of sanctity.

In reading AE's interpretations of the ancient beliefs of Ireland, the thought occurs that the

Druids were quite right in not committing their doctrines to writing. Truth, which awes us by its possibilities as an elemental force, is something less than itself when committed to words, losing its terrors and perhaps even its credibility: and the beliefs of the Druids seem hardly to have been of a kind which lent themselves to definite statement—for instance, the belief, if they had it, as AE says they had, in the ' divinity of Earth ', which appears crude and unrealisable when stated nakedly. Yet conscious life must have originated somehow from the Earth, and to impute divinity to its source would appear a natural extension of the belief in the divine nature of man. The belief, if it was ever held, appears never to have been held generally, perhaps chiefly because the unity men saw was not Earth itself, but the framework of Earth and Heaven, where all frightening and controlling power manifested itself. It was particularly the mystery of man's origin which necessitated some belief of the kind: but very few so far have conceived that the Higher Being to which we are in the relation of created to creator is Earth itself: that the Earth is our God, subordinate to a vaster Being. Yet this is what Russell affirms: ' I believe that most of what was said of God was in reality said of that Spirit whose body is Earth '. The little book was read with admiration for its style by people interested in psychology and particularly in the nature and significance of dreams. Russell himself, as happens to authors who see their fervid imaginations in cold print, soon to some extent lost interest in it, and in a letter to Weekes he expresses surprise that the work has gone into three editions. As a contribution to Irish literature it may stand on the shelf with Yeats's *Celtic Twilight*.

AE's beliefs might be called Pantheism, except that for him the supreme manifestation of being is Earth itself, the Mighty Mother, which is not merely the earth we dig and deface but a spiritual medium in which, as he is fond of quoting, 'We live and move and have our being'. He scouts any approach to an explanation of life and consciousness but the mystical one: reality is perceived with closed eyes. He has no belief in the spontaneous generation of consciousness. All that we think ours, thoughts, imaginations, impulses, come to us from 'a mightier Self of ours, and yet our slave for purposes of its own': they are independent existences, attracted to us according to the nature of our will and aspiration, and he once said that the line of verse into which he had put his essential meaning was: 'All our thoughts are throngs of living souls'. 'Our brain', he asserts,

A Memoir of AE

'is as full of living creatures as our body is thronged with tiny cells, each a life, or as the blood may swarm with bacteria.' 'The moment we close our eyes and are alone with our thoughts and the pictures of dream, we are alone with mystery and miracle. Or are we alone? Are we secure there from intrusion? Are we not nearer the thronged highways of existence, where gods, demons, men and goblins all are psychical visitors?' 'Even in visible nature does not every minutest point of space reflect as a microcosm the macrocosm of earth and heaven?... There is nothing incredible in the assumption that every cell in the body is wrapped about with myriad memories.' By various arguments AE makes his point of view at least comprehensible to us; but the visionary experiences by which he seeks to prove that 'we have access to a memory greater than our own, the treasure-house of august memories in the innumerable being of Earth', will probably be as great a stumbling-block to the ordinary reader as the 'Memorable Relations' are to most readers of Swedenborg.

AE's doctrines are brought into relation to Ireland by his belief in a localised Earth-memory of spiritual happenings, for in his visionary world Druidic Ireland becomes as active a centre of

A Memoir of AE

magical knowledge as Egypt or India. 'A literature so continuously imaginative, visionary and beautiful as the Gaelic would, I do not doubt, have culminated in some magnificent expression of the spirit if life had not been drawn from central depths to surfaces by continuous invasions. I think that meditation is beginning now, and the powers which were present to the ancestors are establishing again their dominion over the spirit.' Fantastic as these beliefs may seem (especially perhaps to Irishmen!) it is of interest to remember that they were firmly held by the man who on various occasions took a prominent part in Irish political happenings, the earnest figure at the Convention, the wise and competent economist, who was certainly regarded by many outside Ireland as its most eloquent and moderate interpreter. There was a point in AE's mind in which the mystical nationalism of Pearse met and blended with these beliefs, and perhaps the Holy Ireland of Pearse's fanatical idealism was not a less incredible fiction than AE's land of Druidic magic. It was a time in Ireland of strange exaltation.

We live in a tolerant age, and AE's mystical philosophy was accepted without inquisition simply as part of himself, and very few of his innumerable friends bothered themselves about it.

A Memoir of AE

16

I remember that one evening when Joseph O'Neill brought the news of the break-up of the German armies, AE would hardly credit it. He had expected the War to end differently, with stalemate and general revolution. And now what would happen in Ireland? At this time he was in great demand as an exponent of the Irish situation, and tells Professor A. Victor Murray (November 1918):

> 'I get requests for lectures about three times a week. This week you, T. P. O'Connor who wants me for Liverpool, and the Labour Party here who want me to speak on the Russian Revolution, make up my average. But if you knew the sickness and loathing of public speech I have, and the positive illness I have when it is a positive duty to do it, you would forgive me. Writing is a poor game, and I don't care much for it either, but it is the only thing I am fit for, because I am a bundle of nerves.'

A new chapter of Irish history began in December with the victory of Sinn Féin in the General Election, and on 21st January, 1919—a memorable date as it turned out—he writes to Weekes:

A Memoir of AE

' Our Sinn Féiners are holding the first meeting of their Assembly to-day in Dublin. I am not specially interested. But I am burrowing underground, mining the soul and preparing explosions for a later date. The coming national policy will be a blend of Pearse, Connolly and AE.'

And now followed the ' Anglo-Irish War '—a real war in the sense that the killing, with due notice given, of selected individuals associated with the maintenance of the British connection, was a method of hostilities at first condoned and finally adopted by militant nationalism. In this turbulent scene, Russell was a distracted figure, disapproval of all violence contending in his mind with anger at the enemy of Ireland's Gaelic soul. In another letter to his friend Weekes, in whom he most confides, he writes :

' I am tied for my sins to movements, and do my best in them, but I am remote from them while I am in them. I will be glad when the call comes to get back to myself, and the great silence swallows me up. If it obliterates me I would not much care.'

1920 was a terrible year, the likeness to a state of war being maintained in the general disposition

A Memoir of AE

to condone deeds of bloodshed, occasionally daring exploits, more often cruel murders, though newspapers were not permitted to call them so. But it was actually accepted as warfare by the British Government when the principle of reprisals was adopted, and gangs of desperate ex-soldiers were introduced as auxiliaries to the defenders of order. Looking back on that time, it seems to me now that Russell had more reason on his side than I then thought, when as we came into town one morning on the top of the tram, we wrangled over the distinction between war and murder. He maintained there was none ; and when I said, I suppose with absurd heat, that this was a defence of murder, he rose and climbed down off the tram, and we did not speak to one another for a good while afterwards. There was a house in Templeogue where we met on Saturday evenings, AE then reading out chapters of his *Interpreters*, and one night, coming to the door and learning I was there, he turned and walked back to Dublin. I stuck to my guns, however, and for a good while he ignored my sidelong glance as we passed in the street, until one day he turned suddenly, and we made it up.

No incident of the struggle moved Russell more than the death of Terence MacSwiney in Brixton Gaol after sixty-nine days' refusal of food, and in an impassioned sonnet, admired as well as deplored by the Unionist papers, he compared MacSwiney to the 'fabled Titan chained upon the hill'. AE's admiration was probably independent of his sympathy with MacSwiney's cause, and it was certainly unaffected by the statements issued after MacSwiney's death of his complicity in various assassinations. What moved AE was the manifestation of human endurance and of 'that within us which can conquer pain': the same feeling which had stirred him as a boy for the 'dying woman', or in the Great War for the 'battle-ecstasy' of heroes on both sides. This sonnet, unlike most of his occasional verse, was included in the Selection from his poems made by him when he was himself a dying man.

It was at least a kind of real warfare when the Black and Tans began to wreck the creameries of the I.A.O.S., on the pretext that they were used as a basis of attack on the military and police. As the creameries were dotted everywhere through the country, there was probably some justification for Sir Hamar Greenwood's assertion in the House of Commons that they were centres of revolutionary propaganda; but Plunkett and Anderson, both good Unionists, were naturally incensed and demanded an enquiry. Russell, of course, was furious, and in a pamphlet, *A Plea for Justice*, he drew up a detailed report of the damage done, estimated at a quarter of a million. In this pamphlet, of which ' many thousands were circulated in Great Britain ', we recognise Plunkett's restraining influence ; yet when some of Russell's statements were quoted in the House of Commons, Sir Hamar Greenwood referred to him as ' an extremist '. A second pamphlet, to which Plunkett contributed, continued to press for an enquiry.

In ' exploring every avenue ' to the solution of the Irish problem, the poet-economist of Rathgar Avenue was remembered in Downing Street, and in November 1920—the month after the culminating horrors of ' Bloody Sunday '—AE was invited over to breakfast with the Prime Minister (24th November). I should have liked to hear AE's personal impressions at this interview, but he would only tell me what he had said to Lloyd George (which unfortunately I have forgotten), and that ' there was cunning in every wrinkle ' in the Premier's face. From a reference in a letter to Yeats, he seems to have suggested to the Premier a policy based on ' playing off ' Ulster by making it believe that it now had the power to bestow on Ireland the great gift of national unity. As he wandered away from Downing Street he thought of something he had not said, and in the free and easy manner of Dublin turned and knocked again at the door of No. 10, only to be told that the Premier was absorbed in business with another visitor. At the interview, Russell undertook to convey some message to Arthur Griffith, then in Mountjoy Gaol, but this seems to have come to nothing. At the end of the year, the first stage of an Irish settlement was reached in the acceptance by Ulster of Home Rule.

It was probably during this visit to London that he called on Northcliffe; and in an article in *Foreign Affairs* ('Twenty-five Years of Irish Nationality'), written after the Irish settlement, he claims indirectly a share, through this interview, in bringing it about :

> ' I was in London for a week during the years of the struggle and sought out Lord Northcliffe, who remembered that he was an Irishman. He asked me, " What can I do to help ? " I said he could bring American opinion to bear upon English opinion, that his vast organisation would enable him to get in touch with the leaders of opinion in the United States. In less than a week he had column after column of American opinions in the papers he controlled, the voice of America's prominent statesmen, lawyers and

industrialists, and it was so unanimous in favour of Irish self-government that I think it was mainly responsible for the feeling which arose in Great Britain that the Irish question was not only a domestic problem but was a world question.'

In January 1921 he writes to Sir William Rothenstein :

'I am trying to live in my mind at present, as to look out of the windows of the body is to invite unpleasant visions in Ireland, so to escape practical politics I am writing about ideal politics in a futurist symposium, " What relation have the politics of time to the politics of eternity ? " in other words, " Why does the Earth Spirit inspire its children in such contrary directions ? " In this symposium I have an ideal nationalist, imperialist, socialist and anarchist, all finding justification for their politics in the Oversoul, and I have tied myself into such knots that the book goes very slowly. However I am in the tenth chapter out of twenty contemplated, and I hope to have it done by the end of the year if I do not come in the path of one of the frequent bullets which travel our streets running after the slow pedestrian.'

A Memoir of AE

The politics of time, indeed, what with murders, kidnappings and explosions, continued during the year to be too exciting to be ignored, and Russell's literary work, besides editing the *Homestead* ('which I don't call writing'), included some vigorous pamphleteering. In *The Inner and the Outer Ireland* his assertion of the purity of Ireland's Gaelic soul is as confident as his assumption that the only considerations which weighed with Unionists were those of material advantage. In another pamphlet, however, *Ireland and the Empire at the Court of Conscience*, he applies the method of *The Interpreters* and dramatises the conflicting political ideals. The occasion was a momentous one. The British Government had suddenly presented the Sinn Féin leaders with the alternative of real war or the acceptance of proposals beyond the wildest dreams and probably even wishes of the great majority of Irishmen. The complete transformation of Irish politics by the Treaty is fortunately not part of our subject: we are concerned only with the part taken in it by AE; and it must be confessed that his pamphlet, of which the purpose was presumably to give some kind of lead to Irish opinion, only reveals the remoteness of his idealism from the actualities of politics. It marshals the arguments on both sides, and then leaves it to the transcendental

A Memoir of AE

wisdom of the National Being to determine the choice. AE's Ireland, in fact, never was on sea or land. It included an Ulster which he always claimed as an Ulsterman to know better than others, yet he seems hardly to have counted on the possibility, in case of the acceptance of the Treaty, that Ulster would not realise that it belonged to his ideal Ireland. One of the organisers of the I.A.O.S., Mr. Robert Bratton, gives us a glimpse of Russell on the evening of the day on which the Treaty was signed:

> ' Sir Horace Plunkett had invited the staff to supper, and I was fortunate enough to be in AE's company on the way out to Foxrock. It was evident that he was greatly pleased, even elated, over the settlement, and gave me the impression that he felt confident no serious difficulties would arise to prevent a complete understanding between Ulster and the rest of Ireland. "What do you think Ulster will do?" he asked. "Ulster will opt out", I replied. It was evident my reply was not what he expected, for he instantly became quite furious with me, and wanted to know on what ground I based my statement. Then without giving me an opportunity to reply he demanded loudly: "What are your political views anyway?"

A Memoir of AE

'I said that everything had got so mixed up in Irish politics that it was difficult for one to define where one stood, but I made it clear that my sympathies at any rate were not Republican. " Anyway, Mr. Russell," I said, " I don't think your question is quite a fair one."

'" Oh, don't you indeed ! Well, I don't give a damn who knows my political views ", he roared, and then lapsed into complete silence.'

The ' National Being ', where it really exists, may certainly be directed by transcendental wisdom, but in times of crisis communities seldom appear to know their own minds, and generally it is some forcible individual, with a will of his own, who makes up their minds for them. In this case it appears to have been Michael Collins, of whose efforts to secure the ratification of the Treaty by the Dáil Russell writes appreciatively to his friend Sir Henry Lawson :

'We might have a really honest administration, though it might be inefficient at first. If Collins is the dominant figure, I think we will get efficiency ; if De Valera, I think we will get inefficiency. Collins is a very remarkable fellow, with a good deal of the mind of a big statesman. Well, a fortnight will make our fate known.

Ireland will be a very interesting place if the Treaty is accepted.'

Seven votes saved Ireland from a war with England, and in the new administration, which was both 'honest' and 'efficient', AE had the satisfaction of seeing his own and Plunkett's ideas of Dominion self-government adopted: the acceptance of the new government being mainly due to the common-sense patriotism of the Unionist part of the population, which made up its mind to support it. AE now declared that Ireland was the least revolutionary country in the world, and had the most stable government. Outside Ireland he was still regarded as Ireland's most representative, as he was certainly its most eloquent, spokesman. In February he delivered an address to the Sociological Society in London, and about the same time a fake interview with him appeared in the American *Century*, which caused him much annoyance.

The year was not far advanced, however, when it began to appear as if a war with England—waged presumably a little good-naturedly by the latter Power—might have saved Ireland a good deal of bloodshed and destruction; and in a letter of July to his friend T. Spicer Simpson he is using his old phrase of the Black-and-Tan period, 'the Devil is

A Memoir of AE

loose in this country'. Sir Henry Wilson was murdered in London in June, and at the same time the Civil War began with the seizure of the Four Courts by Rory O'Connor. The murder of Sean Hales, a Member of the Dáil, was punished by Rory O'Connor's execution; and the same fate befell that strange man Erskine Childers, Russell's friend, for the crime of carrying arms. In August, Michael Collins met his death on a road near Macroom. A long series began of burnings of country mansions, of which that which most directly affected Russell was the blowing-up of Kilteragh, Sir Horace Plunkett's home at Foxrock.

Yet it was during this trying period that he produced *The Interpreters*, a little work which we can imagine some future William James holding up to the admiration of a world in which, according to the supposition of the narrative, ' the thinkers ' have begun to assume of the universe that ' it is a spiritual being '. It is a strange product of that idealism which, fed from various sources, helped to inspire the Insurrection of 1916, and its view of society presents a striking contrast to that of speculators like H. G. Wells, who, leaving out the soul, endeavour to interest us in their picture of a well-managed world centuries hence. But such Utopias belong to the limbo of literature, and the only way to interest man in his future is through some religious conception of it. With AE nothing else but the soul counts; and in this symposium of political dreamers he explains his view of the soul, as Plato explained his in the *Republic*. It makes indeed a tremendous difference if the function of the State is conceived as the education of the soul of man, and if man's faculties of will and intelligence are regarded as the instruments through which he is to achieve his true being.

It is imagined that a world-state has come into being, enforcing its will by aerial armaments, and that in one ancient nation a conspiracy to revolt has been detected, its leaders arrested and thrown together in a room where they await execution. There is a poet-nationalist, like AE himself; an anarchist-individualist; a communist; an artist; an imperialist (arrested by mistake); and an old philosopher, whose part it is to arbitrate in the discussion which arises, after the manner of Socrates. 'As between himself and Heaven', each agrees to lay bare the principles which have led him to revolt. Real dramatic talent is shown in the exposition of conflicting beliefs, having a common origin in the soul of man, and a particularly effective speech is given to the imperialist Heyt (a name probably suggested by that of J. R.

A Memoir of AE

Hecht, a writer with whom AE was at the time in correspondence); while the character who most nearly resembles AE himself, the poet of the National Being, is not allowed to pull more than his own weight in the argument. The scheme of the fantasy is well maintained to the close, where it is a little spoiled by localisation in the introduction of AE's long poem on the Irish Rebellion, ' Michael '.

The conclusion reached is that all the conflicting idealisms are justified and harmonised in the soul of man. The book, however, is really much more of the type of Bunyan's *Holy War* than of Plato's playfully serious imagination, the ' politics of time ' counting for almost as little with AE as the municipal problems of the City of Destruction with Bunyan. AE's world, like Bunyan's, is a sombre world ; and as its darkness is only illumined for Bunyan by gleams from the gates of the Celestial City, so in AE's ' politics of eternity ' life is redeemed by the distant draw which the soul of man experiences towards his ultimate divinity. ' For every man on earth there is a divinity in the heavens who is his Ancestral Self ' ; but ' the will has not yet found its conscious root in the power which sustains the Cosmos '. It is a form of belief in the Fall of Man which, by his own testimony, sprang up in Russell as a boy while he walked in the roads near Armagh, before he had ever heard of Theosophy, which he accepted unquestioningly. His *Homeward: Songs By the Way* were the first hymns of this belief, and *The Interpreters* is a commentary necessary to the understanding of the truths affirmed throughout his poems. These ideas would not be specially interesting here if he had merely derived them from Theosophy, but they appear to have been native to his mind. The unnamed Diotima of the Old Philosopher's wisdom is, however, certainly the authoress of *The Secret Doctrine*.

17

The writing of *The Interpreters* was an excellent preparation for the new task which now awaited him. It might have been expected that his long experience had qualified him to take office under the new Irish government: he was invited to become a Member of the Senate, but refused. Probably he conceived for himself in the new Ireland a part like that of the Old Philosopher in his story, as the friend and admonisher of Irish youth; probably he shared in the general mood of Ireland itself, which, when the British administration withdrew, found it at first a little irksome to shoulder tasks which had hitherto been done for it. Yet it often happens that when we have consciously accepted our lot, and see our way most clearly before us, Destiny chooses that particular moment in which to confront us with some undesired and disconcerting promotion. Thus when it was proposed to Russell that he should become a leader and director of Irish opinion as the editor of a fully equipped journal, modelled on one of the principal London weeklies, he shrank from the new responsibility. He was well satisfied to go on as he was, supplementing his modest income from the *Irish Homestead* by the sale of his pictures: he had never felt the need of money, and his two sons were now young men doing for themselves. But Plunkett was persistent. Plunkett was now an old man, minded to go and live in England: it was as though he had beheld in the flames of Kilteragh a chariot of escape, and before mounting into it he would bestow his mantle on the prophet-companion of so many years. He would leave it to Russell to foster in Ireland that ' public opinion ' which Lecky had declared to be what was lacking in Ireland to make it a nation. He had arranged everything. The *Irish Homestead* was to be incorporated with a new issue of the *Irish Statesman*, and he had

A Memoir of AE

induced a group of American friends to undertake financial responsibility for the new journal. Russell at length yielded, and the *Irish Statesman* began to appear in September 1923.

Plunkett, as already said, had always shown a royal instinct in the choice of persons, and his choice of AE for this work was not the least of his benefactions to Ireland. AE proved a great editor. Looking back through the file of the *Irish Statesman* we might regret that so much vigorous thought and often noble writing should share the inevitable fate of the most brilliant journalism, did we not remember that it brought out all that was best in AE, and called into play all his unmatched abilities. He was assisted by an able journalist from the North of Ireland, J. W. Good, and by the lively and devoted Susan Mitchell, and he now gathered round him a group of brilliant contributors. But a great part of the writing was his own. 'Yes', he tells Miss Grace Jameson in a letter of 1932, 'I was " Y.O. ", also " Querist ", also " O.L.S.", " Gab " and " AE ". When I was editing I had not many collaborators and wrote a great deal myself under different pseudonyms.' 'A man never knows how much work there is in him till he has to do it', was a saying of his. In a single number we find (all written by

A Memoir of AE

himself) well-informed notes on current topics, home and foreign; at least one brilliant leading article; a literary or philosophical 'causerie'; a poem; book-reviews; besides that part of the paper which continued the work of the *Irish Homestead*. Yet this constant mental activity never became with him irksome drudgery, and ideas seemed to troop to his bidding from the aerial fields in which they were at play (as he believed they did). From his editorial vantage-ground he could see along the whole front of Irish nationality and could place his mind at any point at which his attention was demanded. The economic position he understood probably better than anyone; in politics he was chiefly guided by the assumption of Ireland's essential unity, which meant of course that Ireland was an English-speaking community; and his assertion that 'the creation of a Gaelic State is unrealisable, and the ideal of an Irish culture relying on its own resources is impossible', drew a good deal of protest even from his friends.

'I have a very different work to do with the *Irish Statesman* from what I did with its predecessor the *Irish Homestead*,' he writes to Van Wyck Brooks after three months of editorship. 'I have a much wider but a very reactionary audience, and if

A Memoir of AE

the *Irish Statesman* appears to you to be very conservative, it is still advanced compared with Irish daily papers.' He would have preferred to be advocating a new social order and the ' Co-operative Commonwealth ', and his paper was in fact remarkable for a respectful attention to the Russian Revolution and admiration for its leaders. But if he found fault with the new government for being too conservative, it was not without a patriotic satisfaction—when the Civil War died down and things began to go swimmingly in the Free State—that he now spoke of Ireland as the most secure of all countries from revolution. He was taxed with changing his opinions, especially by the redoubtable Miss Mary MacSwiney ; and indeed in his sharp sermons to his countrymen on ' culture and manners ', as well as in the tone of his advice to Labour—now incited to fresh disturbance on the return of Larkin from the United States—it is sometimes hard to recognise the fiery pamphleteer of former years. He supported the Government in its stern repression of armed violence.; and his enthusiastic advocacy of the Shannon Scheme was of considerable service to Cosgrave. He called for education, technical training, libraries ; and when it was proposed to limit Copyright in Ireland to books printed there he offered strenuous

A Memoir of AE

opposition, as later on he exerted himself to defeat the proposed censorship. On one subject his advocacy was somewhat intemperate and scarcely diplomatic, the agitation for the return of the Lane Pictures : a nice question of ethics and legality, as to which perhaps the most significant comment was the silent indifference of the Irish public.

But it was in literature and literary criticism that the chief strength of the *Irish Statesman* lay : indeed it may be said to have effected a new literary revival, in which AE was as much the central figure as Yeats had been in the first. If the morning freshness had passed from the Movement, there was a wider awakening of intelligence, more criticism, a more secure recognition of the part of literature and thought in the national life. It was to the Irish mind generally that the new journal offered an organ of expression, and ingenious speculation and unfettered interchange of opinion were as characteristic of this new phase as lyric and drama had been of the first. The new opportunity, as well as the personality of the editor, brought out the talent of writers hitherto in the background, like the poet Oliver Gogarty and the historian Edmund Curtis ; and besides contributors already well known, a number of new names then coming brightly above the horizon moved through the pages of the *Irish Statesman*. But we are concerned here with Russell and his development. He grew immensely more tolerant, better informed, wiser. The continued attention to new books, new ideas, new personalities exactly suited him. His life entered on a new phase, and the quizzically regarded poet-economist of Plunkett House, with strange notions about the Irish gods and 'the fairies', now became the most noted disseminator of culture in Ireland, or rather in that small proportion of the Irish population which read books. His faculty of rapid yet exhaustive reading—necessary to the critic whose duty it is to grasp the essential purport of many books—together with his amazing memory and talking powers, gave him an advantage over slower minds, and, especially at his Sunday evening gatherings, he acquired the ascendancy of a minor Dr. Johnson. This comparison occurred to one of his circle, C. P. Curran, whose eloquent description of him at this period, when he was the real centre of Dublin's intellectual life, indicates also that he had something of the maieutic art of Socrates :

'He made no difference of persons : the latest and youngest new-comer had his attention as if he were the long-awaited Avatar. The variety

A Memoir of AE

of his conversation was a Dublin proverb, ranging over philosophy, economics and the arts. The matter of his talk was copious and richly illustrated ; his dialectic resourceful and dexterous ; its temper beyond all praise. A kindly wisdom throned over debate, comprehending and all-forgiving. The most divergent opinions found patient hearing, but the immoderate appeared a little ridiculous.' (*Studies*, September 1935.)

AE in his last years was not unaware that he had put a large part of himself into this fugitive form of periodical literature, and just before his death he wrote to his son in America, suggesting that if a selection should be made the proper person to undertake it was his young friend, Monk Gibbon. This task has now been carefully performed in the ample volume entitled *The Living Torch* (Macmillan).

For all his writing he had the same style available, and this explains the absence of any strong personal interest in his private letters. There is no intimate revelation of what is going on behind the scenes in his private life. In his flawless moral nature there were no concealments, none of that fun in playing a part in life which sometimes pleases us in the

A Memoir of AE

printed correspondence of public men. Was this the 'essential humour' in which George Moore said he was lacking? Was he not rogue enough for a man of letters? Certainly his letters seldom enable us to supplement our presentation of the man who appears in his published writings, at all events in his prose. Yet it is a vigorous and fluid medium, this prose which he has at command, pouring it forth, as readily as in one of his articles, in a long letter to a friend, which he will set about writing while perhaps he is waiting for proofs. Here, for instance, is part of a letter to Seán O'Faoláin (November 1926):

'I note you have been reading Spengler. His philosophy of history is exciting and interesting, but I always feel life much more complicated than even Spengler would make it out to be, and that generalisations on history which seem when you read the book to be sound, the moment you turn from the book and make original observations for yourself you discover that you could make another generalisation the exact opposite of the one about which you have been reading and could get ample evidence to prove it so. I think myself that the reactions do not take place within such long periods of time but begin at once; that the moment one powerful idea is made manifest, at that very moment the opposite idea or energy is called into being, and they go on warring in society; " one lives the other's death, one dies the other's life ". Some followers of Spengler, because there has been such a development of engineering and mechanics, think that life itself has become mechanical, whereas I believe there was never more freedom of thought than there is at present, and that the moulds of mind of serfs under the feudal system were much more a prison for the soul than the moulds of mind of mechanics in, let us say, one of Henry Ford's factories. I have no evidence to bring, but I think my proposition is arguable.'

And two days later he writes to Mrs. Fiske Warren:

' I have been reading *The Travelling Philosopher* for the past two weeks and I am really grateful to you for the gift of these extraordinary volumes. I think Keyserling has a richer and deeper culture and a wider power of sympathy and interpretation of the spiritual ideas of others than any writer I know. I know a good deal about Indian religions, as they have been the main object of my meditations since I was twenty, and I was astonished to find subtleties comprehended I think in a way no other European writer has been able to match. His observations on national character are stimulating, but his greatest gift to his readers is his own sympathetic personality. I find myself led out of moulds in which my mind had been congesting and set free to think in a wider aether than before. I have not for fifteen or twenty years read a book which interested me more, and after reading it rather hastily to get a general impression of the book, I intend to take up in detail passages which I have marked for deeper consideration. The only part of the Diary which disappointed me was the American part. I think he found the cultural life of the United States so completely outside his sympathies that the pages dealing with them are vague generalities without the precision of his chapters on India or China. I think in U.S.A. he found himself, the highly subtle and cultivated mind, in a society which to him appeared altogether crude, and his stay was not long enough or he had not introduction to the most cultivated Americans who might have helped to interpret the New World to him. I wished he could have met somebody like Lewis Mumford whose *Sticks and Stones* and *The Golden Day* I have been reading with much delight, for I think books like these would have given Keyserling some kind of starting point from which he could have approached American culture. He seems fortunate in those he met in China and in India. Though I think Annie Besant and Leadbeater are poor interpreters of Indian religions, he seems to have slipped by them to the true fountains, and they appear merely as straws blowing in the same path he was treading, and his meditation is his own not theirs. Keyserling is the only author I have read for years whom I would like to meet. I divine things in him deeper perhaps than anything he has written. Probably in his attempts at Yogi concentration he got to depths which he did not refer to, as I think he only writes about ideas which have become rationalised in his nature, and the half intelligible gleams and vistas attained in meditation, though coming out of a deeper life than his normal, did not lend themselves to that rationalising and subtle intellect which is spiritual but yet always seeks lucidity. I am truly grateful for this book, which I will treasure as I do Goethe's " Conversations with Eckermann" because there is the same rich, subtle and many-sided personality in them and I love the rich mind more than anything else.'

Passages like these, interesting in themselves, might be multiplied from AE's letters, but I will limit myself to those which indicate some movement in his life and mind. The following may be quoted from a letter of this time to Van Wyck Brooks:

'We in Ireland are reacting against the idealism which led us to war, and I fear we are in for an era of materialism. Our new Government is, however, honest and energetic, and from a romantic conception of Ireland is being unrolled the idea of the highly efficient modern state. I should like to live for fifteen years more, because I think we will react again to the imaginative and spiritual, and we shall probably begin a fight for spiritual freedom. But Ireland is a very small and unimportant part of the planet, and I don't share the egomania of my countrymen who think the whole world is staring at them. But it is a lovely country to live in.'

What the effect has been on the Irish mind generally of the achievement of self-government I am unable to judge, but it is certain that the effect on AE was to abate the intensity of his nationalism. He now called himself an internationalist, and was presently to tell an American audience:

A Memoir of AE

'I have met the hundred per cent Irish and the hundred per cent English and the hundred per cent American, and I have always wondered why these perfect embodiments of their nation were the most perfectly intolerable people, at least from the artist's and poet's point of view.[1]

18

This on the whole was AE's great period, and even his old friend Weekes could hardly lament that he was not a 'success'. The acknowledged 'seer of the rural community' and prophet of the Co-operative Commonwealth, he was also in high estimation as a poet and artist, and now he was a noted instructor of public opinion and a critic whose reviews were more and more looked for by the new writers. But above all there was what he had made of himself: he was all that a man should be, 'edel, hülfreich, gut'; within his limits, AE was as perfect as Socrates. Yet the fame of his talents, and the still more seductive fame of his virtues, had left the original simplicity and spontaneity of his nature entirely uncontaminated. He was especially beloved by women, as no doubt the

---

[1] Lectures entitled 'The Sunset of Fantasy'.

A Memoir of AE

best men are; the best account of him is a woman's, Madame Simone Téry's essay in *L'Île des bardes*, as remarkable for its glowing picture of the man in the midst of his circle as for its careful and accurate elucidation of AE's beliefs and principles. Seeing him about the streets, it occurred to one sometimes to wonder whether there was not a special significance for Ireland in the appearance of this unique Believer in the midst of its troubles, and in particular for Ireland's inchoate, half-alien capital, nurse and mother of famous men. These for the most part have fled from it, but Russell (a Dubliner indeed only by adoption) remained. Dublin, where there is much architectural provision for the soul, is somehow not a place in which the soul has been discovered: was it the mission of AE to discover the soul for this city? Certainly, the one outcome from the troubles which he hoped and looked for was the discovery of the soul; and he had been the real prophet of that national mysticism associated with the Rising of 1916. Russell's beliefs, however, were not regarded very seriously by his fellow-townsmen, who did not even think it worth while to inform themselves accurately as to their nature. He was supposed to believe in 'the fairies'; a harmless belief, which even in times and places in which heresies aroused grave attention would

A Memoir of AE

hardly have brought him to the grim predicament of Socrates. A few thought of AE in a part more suited to his character : ' The little town of Lurgan in which he was born ', writes St. John Ervine, ' is notorious in Ireland for the harshness of its religious discussions. A base bigotry flourishes there. It is in the nature of things that from a place of great bitterness should come a man of reconciliation, bidding Protestant and Catholic to meet, not in Geneva or in Rome, but on the Holy Hills of Ireland, under the protection of the ancient gods.'

A good many of Russell's friends, who have taken an interest in this record of his life, have counselled me to leave out Theosophy and Madame Blavatsky as much as possible. Why dwell on this aspect of a man whose greatest friends cared least about Karma and Reincarnation, and who delighted to meet all men on their own ground ? And in fact he told Simone Téry that ' what is called Theosophy nowadays is mostly humbug ' ; and he disliked Mrs. Besant's publications almost as much as those of the Catholic Truth Society. Undoubtedly his detachment from the Theosophic Organisation, and especially his withdrawal from it as early as 1898, gave pain to his old companions : yet more than one of these have urged me to

A Memoir of AE

remember that AE was before all things a Theosophist. Whether a Theosophical Council would have accepted all his beliefs as orthodox is doubtful. It was impossible to think of him otherwise than as a free spirit. Yet if he preferred the company of George Moore and Oliver Gogarty to that of the faithful, he was only claiming the privilege of the great believers, who have usually excited adverse comment by the company they kept. And though in the *Irish Statesman* he wrote a caustic notice of 'The Mahatma Letters', it is certain that his loyalty to Madame Blavatsky remained unshaken. In a letter written from London to Seán O'Faoláin a month before his death, he says:

'You dismiss H. P. Blavatsky rather too easily as "hocus pocus". Nobody ever affected the thought of so many able men and women by "hocus pocus". The real source of her influence is to be found in *The Secret Doctrine*, a book on the religions of the world suggesting or disclosing an underlying unity between all great religions. It was a book which Maeterlinck said contained the most grandiose cosmogony in the world, and if you read it merely as a romantic compilation, it is one of the most exciting and stimulating books written for the last hundred

A Memoir of AE

years. It is paying a poor compliment to men like Yeats, Maeterlinck, and others, to men like Sir William Crookes, the greatest chemist of modern times, who was a member of her society, to Carter Blake, F.R.S., the anthropologist, and the scholars and scientists in many countries who read H. P. Blavatsky's books, to assume that they were attracted by "hocus pocus". If you are ever in the National Library, Kildare Street, and have a couple of hours to spare, you might dip into "The Proem" to *The Secret Doctrine*, and you will understand the secret of the influence of that extraordinary woman on her contemporaries. I found in a publication of the Oxford Press, *The Thibetan Book of the Dead*, a statement made by Samdip Lal, who was the greatest Sanskrit and Thibetan scholar in the world, that H. P. Blavatsky was one of the very, very few Europeans who have a mastery over Indian philosophy and mysticism. You have the makings of an admirable literary critic, a rare thing in these times, and you should not be misled by popular catchwords about "hocus pocus", but try to find out the real secret of H. P. Blavatsky's influence, which still persists strong as ever, as I have found over here [in London] among many intellectuals and well-known writers.'

A Memoir of AE

It was AE's belief that during the period beginning 1875 and ending with the death of Judge, there had been a diffusion of spiritual light. After that ' the Theosophical Movement overflowed from the Theosophical Society, and I think better work can be done by Theosophists in working in other movements and imparting to them a spiritual tendency '.[1]

AE's debt to Theosophy was in fact something like that of Blake to Swedenborg. From the first he had understood Theosophy in a way of his own, and in *The Candle of Vision* and *Song and its Fountains* he seems at least as much concerned in making a contribution to literature as to Theosophic thought. A frequent saying of his is correctly reported by George Moore in *Salve* : ' The fault I find with Christianity is that it is no more than a code of morals, whereas three things are required of a religion—a cosmogony, a psychology and a moral code '. Of these three the most important was the first, the psychic as well as the ethical individuality being determined by the stage reached in its ascent. And for AE individuality is a state of self-imposed exile : over each human soul stands its archetype, what he calls the Ancestral Self, a blissful perfection which it has renounced—as is shadowed forth in the

[1] Article by P. G. Bowen in *The Aryan Path*, December 1935.

A Memoir of AE

myth of the rebel angels—entering for the sake of experience on the ' pilgrimage of pain ' and nursing its power once more to ' storm the heavens '. The gods are ourselves, as we have been and as we shall be again when we have returned ' Homeward '. The Ancestral Self is the Oversoul of each human entity. The individual is not by itself an immortal entity but ' comes to its immortal ' ; just as in youth (and here AE's experience seems very different from that of Wordsworth in his ' Ode ') we are at first an inherited animal soul, until, generally about the time of puberty, with the coming of the spiritual soul we enter into our full inheritance of life, with a renewed opportunity of advance. One sublime privilege belongs to every human being, that of entering during ' deep sleep ' into one's ' own immortal ', whence come the true 'intimations of immortality'; and could the waking soul possess the knowledge which it reclaims in that state the purpose of life would for it have been fulfilled. But for this, man must be born again, many times.

A cold uncanny creed all this may seem for men and women! Yet AE found in it the theme of most of his poetry, and no man remembered more constantly than he the ' imperial palace whence he came '. It was a consistent view of life and the

A Memoir of AE

universe, entering into all his sociology as well as his poetry, and his faith in it never wavered, from the days when he described his conception of Evolution in a boyish letter to his first friend, Carrie Rea : 'There must have been a great primeval revelation of all knowledge when the human race began to emerge from the beast, perhaps an incarnation of many Aeons to teach this knowledge'. And it was not inconsistent with a receptive curiosity about all new scientific and philosophic speculation. For him, indeed, the true theology would have been science, converted through the discovery of a purpose in the universe.

Abnormal powers or faculties, such as are often claimed by, or imputed to, believers in occultism, did not play much part in AE's life. It was said that he occasionally produced a certain awe in people by telling them things about their private life and circumstances of which he could not have been told, and I can believe this, having been present when he showed remarkable divination in such things as hand-reading (though he attached little importance to such things). He believed firmly that certain 'magnetic centres' of the Earth-Being were located in Ireland, and in the possibility, especially in these places, of entering into the Earth-Memory ; a psychic region, in which the

A Memoir of AE

forms he beheld seemed to have some kind of objective existence, as though what has been, still is. Whether visionaries like Blake and AE (both artists in whom the visualising faculty may be assumed to have been unusually strong) or Swedenborg (for whom the fine arts did not exist) were entirely deluded by their visions, is perhaps the same problem as that of the nature of dreams which exercised Russell much in his later years. Many of his letters which I have received relate to this subject, but they do not add anything to what he has written in *The Candle of Vision* and *Song and its Fountains*.

Madame Simone Téry reports him as saying:

'What I know is little. I have discovered that consciousness can exist outside the body, that we can sometimes see people who are far away from us, that we can even speak to them when they are hundreds of miles distant : I have been spoken to myself in this way. I know by experience that disembodied beings may act on us profoundly. Life has been poured into me by one of them, and while it lasted I seemed to be scourged with electricity. I am convinced that I remember past lives, and I have spoken with friends who remembered them equally : we have even talked together of places where we lived. I have also seen elemental beings, and people with me have seen them at the same time.'

A letter to Weekes of December 1932 gives his views of death:

'I think about death in numberless ways, for there are numberless gates for us through death. Body to earth, soul to God, is not enough for our being, compounded out of so many previous lives. One part of me shall go back to earth, another part to the illusion of Heaven, another part to its own being—what you think of as Deity—another part perhaps to faery or elemental spheres, for we have all forms of being in ourselves. Our nature, what the Vedic seers called " true own being ", in the prism of nature was dramatically sundered into many-coloured lives, yet all part of ourselves. The rays spread and then gather again. But why write in so few words about what it would take months to elucidate ? I believe I shall live hereafter because I have lived before, and I came upon knowledge of past religions, lives and loves in meditation— found others who knew the same things as I did and who remembered the places where we lived. I went inwards as much as I went outward, and

A Memoir of AE

I was not content to think only but made adventure inward by resolute will, and at times I left this world behind me. I am, in a sense, at peace, believing there is a deep justice in the nature of things, and in another sense I am full of awe and fears because there are such mighty and terrible things in the universe, and we must meet and cope with them all. But I will meet nothing until I am strong enough to come into the sphere of things now above me. I must have evolved in myself more likeness or identity of nature before I can see into a heaven-world or a God-world. You see, I am at once at peace and fearful. . . . I feel my own death will be unworthy because I will go out through the falling-in of walls of clay, whereas I should by the will have before this been able to find a secret radiant gateway into the spirit and gone out by my own will, and not been forced out.'

19

The only thing in life that Russell really cared about was his poetry. The world which he knew and loved, because he had made it, was his own verse-world, and as Providence watches over all its

A Memoir of AE

sparrows, so AE knew and loved every line that he had written. Contrasting himself in this respect with Yeats, he writes to Miss Grace Jameson (1932) : 'If Yeats has written a lyric during the day and at night wishes to speak it for me, he has to read it from his MS. I remember every verse I wrote, and could, if my *Collected Poems* were destroyed, dictate them all without change.' Only as a poet was it possible to think of AE as vain; and I remember, during my early acquaintance with him, almost recoiling from him when he said, after acknowledging the beauty of a poem of Wordsworth that I had submitted to him : 'Of course, I believe that all Wordsworth ever wrote was nothing compared with things I have written!' In other things he was not vain : it was nothing to him, for instance, that he could set the stupid fellows from England right about economics and politics. It was in his poems that he felt truly himself; and as a poet he felt the equal of any : witness the tone of his 'Open Letter' to Kipling on the question of 'Ulster' in 1912. He often mentioned, as of importance, that his poems were 'all conceived and written in the open air. I think that in *Collected Poems* there was only one short lyric which was written while I was in a room' (letter to Weekes). Just before his last

A Memoir of AE

illness I had written a short account of his life and work, not I think an unfair one, yet hardly in the somewhat extravagant vein of eulogy to which he was accustomed, and I was a little concerned about what he would think of it. But he wrote to thank me: I had praised his poetry, which was 'all he cared about'.

Was he justified in this self-confidence? (Amongst the poets, Wordsworth and Tennyson were notorious for the same foible, if it is one: Shelley being the only one of whom it is told that he hated to see again what he had once written.) There is an exactness in likening a true poet to a star—'Shine, poet, in thy place and be content': for the poet who, in whatever region of experience he is placed, converts life into song, is really like a star; for instance, whoever wrote the *Dies Irae* occupies as fixed a place in the poetic heavens as the author of *A Midsummer Night's Dream*. The former of these poets may have been a very different person from what we imagine of him, and may have known the George Moores and artists of his and Dante's time, who perhaps valued his company without suspecting in him the power of frightening the world with that last trumpet-blast of Latin poetry. I am reminded of him now, because AE in his apocalyptic vein is really more akin to him than to the many-mooded, often over-clever and sometimes positively half-crazy poets of his own period. Take for example a poem of which it might be said—as Coleridge said of certain lines that if he had met them running wild in the deserts of Arabia he would have exclaimed, 'Wordsworth!'—that it could have been written by no one but AE:

> Not by me these feet were led
>   To the path beside the wave,
> Where the naiad lilies shed
>   Moonfire o'er a lonely grave.
>
> Let the dragons of the past
>   In their caverns sleeping lie.
> I am dream-betrayed, and cast
>   Into that old agony.
>
> And an anguish of desire
>   Burns as in the sunken years,
> And the soul sheds drops of fire
>   All unquenchable by tears.
>
> I, who sought on high for calm,
>   In the Everliving find
> All I was in what I am,
>   Fierce with gentle intertwined;
>
> Hearts which I had crucified
>   With my heart that tortured them;
> Penitence, unfallen pride—
>   These my thorny diadem!

A Memoir of AE

Thou would'st ease in heaven thy pain,
    O, thou fiery, bleeding thing !
All thy wounds will wake again
    At the heaving of a wing.

All thy dead with thee shall rise,
    Dies Irae. If thy soul
To the Everliving flies,
    There shall meet it at the goal

Love that Time had overlaid,
    Deaths that we again must die—
Let the dragons we have made
    In their caverns sleeping lie.[1]

What this poem means, I do not exactly know, but an incomprehensible poem may take possession of the mind when we have confidence in the author. A good deal of recent poetry seems to be addressed

---

[1] 'That there is no escape from the law of retribution is the theme of the poem " Resurrection ". We must give redress to all those whom in this or any former existence we may have wronged, we must come to peace with those we have hated and opposed. There is no escaping into heaven and thus evading the law of retribution ; for even there the soul would find no peace. All its wounds would wake again at the heaving of a wing. The poet feels some warning voice bidding him not to probe further into his experience nor to stir up what may be memories of wrongs done and left unexpiated in a former existence.' W. M. Clyde, *AE : Poet, Essayist, Painter* (1935).

A Memoir of AE

to a posterity which will understand it better than we do ourselves; and of AE too it may be said that if the anticipation of *The Interpreters* should be realised and there should come a time in which it is 'supposed of the universe that it is a spiritual being', his poetry may assume an importance greater than is allowed it now as a mere contribution to imaginative literature.

He might have shone contentedly, and perhaps more conspicuously, in his place as the author of a score or so of challenging poems, but he was human enough to have literary ambition, and aspired to a place among the poets of his time. The inevitable comparison is with Yeats; and it is a proof of the strength in him of an original poetic impulse that although Yeats was in some respects his poetic master, his voluminous verse shows a striking independence of the Yeats influence, so evident in most of his Irish and in many of his English contemporaries. By sedulous practice he developed and perfected a dignified and lofty diction which he could direct at will on personal and topical themes, but it is never the subtle medium through which the absolute artist enters into and becomes the object of his contemplation. He is eloquent and declamatory—he has even been called 'an Irish Swinburne'. In his epic fragment 'The

A Memoir of AE

House of the Titans', which recalls *Hyperion*, and in the Browningesque 'Dark Lady', he is a brilliant improvisator. His true claim is of a more private nature; and as we read, in *Song and its Fountains*, the stories of his visions, and of the impulses which broke into poems in his mind, we feel that criticism should be silent. It is best for his claims that we should regard him as a religious poet; and as religion is not merely a vague emotion, but a definite regimentation of men's minds into 'varieties of experience', each with peculiarities justifying a particular name, to call him a Theosophical poet, the poet of Theosophy. This may seem to limit unduly his claims as a poet, but there is no question of anything unworthy of AE in his association with a Movement which, at all events in his own generation, was probably the principal agent in the reawakening of the religious instinct. Nor is it without significance for Theosophy that it has 'produced' or attracted to itself a poet. A noble feeling for the divine 'hero' in man breathes through his poems:

> Something beneath yon coward gaze
> Betrays the royal line.

But it is consolation rather than encouragement that is imparted by the poems, which in general

A Memoir of AE

convey a sense of profound sadness. AE's life was a fairly happy one, though he experienced life's ordinary trials (I remember, in the early days of his married life, meeting him at a railway station, when he brushed away a tear as he mentioned, before turning to other subjects, that he had just come from burying his first infant). The pain and 'anguish' which are his constant theme spring, however, from a religious perception of the tragic humiliation of that fallen Titan, Mankind, in this 'Iron Age'; and so genuine is his compassion for human suffering that many readers have drawn consolation from his poems.

'I am glad', he says in a letter to Seán O'Faoláin, 'that you like "We must pass like smoke". Mrs. Watts, the wife of the artist, once wrote me that in an illness in which her life was despaired of, she murmured this poem to herself, and she said it carried her through her illness. That is the commendation of my poetry I treasure. Captain Shaw told me that when he was lying in the trenches at Gallipoli, he used to repeat to himself the poem "Reconciliation" to keep his soul alive; and I once received a letter signed jointly by the father and mother of a young man who died in Thanet, and they

A Memoir of AE

told me that their son through a long illness kept my *Collected Poems* beside him and derived great consolation from them, and read them even on the day of his death. I really tried to write poetry as if I were on the slopes of death myself and was testing my thought by that consciousness ; and that people nigh death or in danger of it should find my poetry coming into their thought, this pleased me more than all the praise in English or American reviews.'

Testimonies to the deep emotion with which certain of his poems were read might be multiplied. Two Viceroys of India were amongst his admirers, the Earl of Lytton and Lord Curzon : of the latter it is told that during an illness in 1917 he consoled himself with AE's poems.

20

A thing to admire in AE was that in his exemplary life there was no conscious exercise of a ' mission '. He seemed to be possessed of some inner self which looked on at his own various activities without lending itself to any of them ; how otherwise he found time for reading and thinking, or for the meditations which constituted

A Memoir of AE

his devotional life, it was hard to say, for he was in his office all day, and for each evening of the week (except Sundays, when he received visitors, and Thursdays, when he presided at the Hermetic Society) there was some house which he visited regularly. And he talked perpetually. 'I think', Edmund Curtis once said reflectively, 'Russell must have spoken more *words* than almost anybody.' Mary Devenport O'Neill, wife of Joseph O'Neill, the novelist, kindly contributes some notes of his weekly visits to their house :

'He came to see us every Saturday night, and was the merriest of people, radiating vitality and fun. He would describe amusingly the people who had visited him during the week, what was said and what might have been said if he were not a serious editor. He would invent a collaboration between dissimilar authors and give a rough sketch of the result; or weird plots for thrillers, urging one or other of us to write them. He never attempted to write them himself : " At one time I might have done it ", he would say. It was surprising to find the number of things he was interested in and knew a good deal about, even boxing and football; and if film stars were mentioned he could say what they were best in. There was always a political discussion with my husband, and then he would ask what we had been reading. . . . He was at first prejudiced against the Russian novelists because of their lack of a traditional culture, but we persuaded him to try them, and he read the great novels one after another at a tremendous rate, and was moved particularly by Dostoevsky's *House of the Dead*. *The Three Musketeers* was undoubtedly his favourite book, and if he even thought of it he had to tell the story of it all over again. But if asked what his favourite book was he would I think have said *John Inglesant*. The best detective story, he constantly said, was *The Bishop Murder Case* by Van Dine.

' One Saturday night when I was away, my husband, who had been tramping the mountains, arrived home wanting a meal, and there was no one to give it to him. He found mutton cutlets and cold boiled potatoes in the larder, and taking them to the kitchen he had started clumsily to try to turn them into food, when he heard AE's unmistakable knock. He mentioned what had happened, not expecting more than a vague sympathy, but to his surprise AE grew business-like at once and came quickly

A Memoir of AE

to the kitchen. "But, man, you don't need all that grease in the pan. Get me a bowl; I must pour off three-fourths of it. Slice those potatoes while I cook the cutlets." And with a professional skill AE cooked them, while my husband tried to follow his instructions.'

He stood 5 ft. 11 in. and was well-proportioned, with a russet-bearded countenance in which kindliness was the prevailing expression. The brow was neither wide nor lofty, and was hidden in a tangle of mouse-coloured hair, never trimmed except by himself, for when he decided it was too long he went at it himself with scissors in front of a glass. All the power of the head (this is brought out specially in Donald Gilbert's bust of him) was in the large full face, with high cheek-bones giving him the look of a countryman of Dostoevsky, and a pugnacious mouth disclosing large teeth discoloured by tobacco. Quizzical blue-grey eyes twinkled behind his glasses, and the whole appearance was extraordinarily winning: some even called him handsome. A huge tie proclaimed the artist, his clothes being always slack and shabby. In his earlier years he was straight and slim, and I remember admiring his lithe figure as he stood stripped for diving; but in his fifties he began to

A Memoir of AE

grow corpulent and moved heavily, and during his last illness at Bournemouth, when he asked me to get him some collars, I had to try in several shops before finding one that would go round his great neck.

He spoke with a decided Ulster accent, in a mellow musical voice, and persisted in certain pronunciations, 'laughture', 'prĕtty', 'murning' (for 'mourning'), etc. Apropos of George Moore's remark that he 'lacked the essential humour', it may be mentioned that he never really laughed, though at anything that tickled him he would go off into a chuckle. Needless to say, he was careless about food and wasted no time over his meals; he enjoyed an imperturbable digestion, and his pipe was his constant companion.

A great sorrow befell him in March 1926 when Susan Mitchell died. 'This was the only time', Mary Devenport O'Neill writes, 'that I saw AE troubled emotionally (I was away when Mrs. Russell died). His natural optimism had received a bad blow. He sat there trying to talk of things as usual, but he gave the impression of being emptied of content, almost like a person who had lost a lot of blood. It was a revelation to us.' Two years afterwards he wrote to his old friend Mrs. Coates (Carrie Rea):

A Memoir of AE

'Though I have of all I know the most confident belief in immortality, yet none the less I found myself affected by death as if there were no hereafter. For two years I kept mourning day after day the death of a dear friend who I could yet feel was living, and whose affection seemed to pour on me from beyond the gates of death.'

Miss Mitchell's place in the office was taken by his son Diarmuid, who writes : 'For the first time then I got to know father. He had not hitherto taken much notice of me.'

Susan Mitchell's death was the first real break-up in his life ; and it was probably the need of some distraction which disposed him this year to yield to the persuasions of his friends the Currans to join them in a short visit to Paris. Mr. Curran kindly contributes an account of this expedition :

'He had always maintained that Donegal had more for him than anything France or Italy could offer. But in the autumn of 1926, the franc being low, Helen and I had arranged our holidays for Burgundy, and baiting our hooks with the presence in Paris not merely of Monet but of Simone Téry and James Stephens, we induced him to meet us, returning from the

A Memoir of AE

south and undertaking on our part to relieve him of the worries of foreign travel. With Simone Téry and James Stephens we met him accordingly at the Gare du Nord in September and lodged him with us at the Hôtel Voltaire, Quai du Louvre. It was an entertaining experiment for all of us. I knew that for AE the visible world hardly existed except as the raw material for paint. I knew his indifference to the facts of history and to all institutions, I knew his antipathy to the Renaissance (except Leonardo and Michael Angelo) and to everything that derived from it, to the luxury-art of the eighteenth century and generally to all pomp and circumstance. But none the less I did hope that the aspect of a strange capital and of a new way of living might shake him a little from his subjective base, and implored him to hold his principles and prejudices in suspense for a little while to give his eyes a chance. It was quite useless. He knew himself precisely what he wanted. He wanted to see certain pictures and talk with his friends. Everything else went by the board. I need hardly say that wine and good cooking were thrown away on him, and in café or restaurant he would as soon sit with his back to the street or the crowd as face them. His disregard, as a rule, of immediate surroundings tempted us to let him light his pipe—without the prudent interval—with government matches, but even that lesson was wasted on him. The entire architecture of Paris was less in his eyes than the little *cour* of the *Cheval Blanc* associated in literary legend with D'Artagnan—you remember how he loved Dumas.

But what *did* he appreciate? He liked the wide skies, spaces and vistas that Paris so prodigally affords. Each morning before the *corvée* of sight-seeing began, before the *bouquinistes* had opened their boxes, he would be out on the quai with the sketching-book and chalks he always carried, revelling in the morning light along the river: and Paris never was so captivating as in that haze of grey and silver. He liked the great basin in the Luxembourg gardens where the children sail their boats; the stained glass in the Sainte Chapelle, a long day on the water at Versailles, leaving the Palais carefully unvisited; the view during dinner with Mrs. Cornelius Sullivan from the Butte Montmartre, when the darkening valley between the two hills grew starred with the lights of Paris; another evening in the Bois with the same charming hostess when the lights in the trees and the dancers turned the Pré-Catalan into a Monti-

A Memoir of AE

celli—as a matter of fact he had confessed his anxiety to see people dance amongst restaurant tables as they do at the cinema. And then the pictures. Viewing a gallery with AE was always exciting. His judgments were swift and decisive, always coherent and—given his viewpoint—wholly intelligible. He went through rooms looking for his property, with the rapidity of a globe-trotter, discarding all else but quick to recognise even in the discards a few inches of beauty or an accomplished passage of painting. His concentration was fully exercised and his memory, as always, extraordinarily retentive. Of the old masters in the Louvre he was held most by Fra Angelico's " Coronation of the Blessed Virgin " and a long way after, by the Watteaus. Poussin he accepted, it seemed to me, with some reluctance. Amongst the moderns in the Louvre, and elsewhere in the public galleries and private collections like Durand-Ruel's, he made the closest study of Monet and Rousseau, was interested, for the time being, anyhow, in Gustave Moreau, but Monet remained his abiding admiration. In painting he looked first for the dream, the record of some visionary beauty, then he was concerned with the technical rendering of light.

A Memoir of AE

Monet went a good way towards filling his bill.

We did not go much to the theatre—only once to the Comédie des Champs Élysées then under Jouvet's management, where we saw the revival of Prosper Mérimée's *Le Carrosse du Saint Sacrement*, a graceful and brilliant bit of sophistication appealing to his sense of colour and light.

And then talk—floods of it—not stimulated so much by any new experience as by association with old friends—at dinner and after midnight with James Stephens, at Spicer Simpson's, the American medallist who had done an admirable relief of AE, and at Simone Téry's apartment, where a duel in the recitation of verse was engaged in—the alexandrines of Racine and Baudelaire's grave sonorities pitted against AE's favourites, Ferguson's *Fairy Thorn* and Yeats.'

A visit to Paris might have been important for Russell in his earlier years: it was what friends like Sir Hugh Lane had always desired for him; and many believed that if he had devoted himself from the first to the study and practice of art he would have achieved greatness. The merely technical accomplishment of some water-colours, dated 1885, shown in the Memorial Exhibition held in Dublin after his death, attracted much attention. And as against George Moore's gibes at 'the Donegal Dauber', and other critical disparagement, we must remember that many eminent judges have held a very different opinion of his powers. He had now long ceased to hold his annual exhibitions—the last was in 1913—and anyone who wanted one of his pictures had to seek him out at his house, where he passed his Sunday mornings in elaborating the sketches made during his holidays. The truth was that AE never regarded his painting as having anything like the importance of his writing. Painting was his pastime, writing he believed to be his calling.

'Do you like writing as well as painting?' he asks Sir William Rothenstein. 'I don't, though I can't paint or draw otherwise than as an untaught amateur. When I write my best poem there is nothing to look at except bad handwriting. The lust of the eye is not satiated. But if I paint, something begins to glow and glow under my fingers, and my ignorance of painting prevents my knowing just how bad it is.'

And he tells the same friend :

'I have always been more concerned about the psychology of my imaginations than in trying to write or paint them, and I hope to make those who read feel a more profound interest in imagination and vision, and I hope what I write will react on the arts.'

21

Meanwhile, in the *Irish Statesman* he was as wise and brilliant as ever. A tragic event on which he had to comment in July 1927 was the assassination of Kevin O'Higgins, whom he held to be the master-spirit of Irish politics, or ' chief moral architect of the Free State ' ; and it was followed by the death of his old friend Constance Markievicz, of the party which had brought about O'Higgins's death. To each he paid a fitting tribute ; indeed the fact that the *Irish Statesman* stood outside all parties limited its effectiveness as a journal. Its real achievement was to bring Irish writers together, and it was probably the feeling that there were purely cultural interests and causes which might be advanced through organisation which suggested to W. B. Yeats about this time his project of an

A Memoir of AE

Irish Academy of Letters. The *Statesman* was the organ in which the return of the Lane Pictures could be advocated, or in which the new censorship could be resisted; it was the organ of those who, interested chiefly in the ideas animating literature, politics and social science, are called nowadays in each country its 'Intellectuals'. But alas! it had become evident that this class was not sufficiently numerous or influential in Ireland to support a journal of the high standard maintained by the *Irish Statesman*. Plunkett's American friends, who had subsidised the enterprise, had expected to hear in it the exultant voice of the new Irish nation. But 'the anti-Treaty group were outraged that the paper upheld the Anglo-Irish settlement, and the pro-Treaty group denounced its half-heartedness in dealing with the Republican extremists. The North objected to its appeal for Irish unity as strenuously as the South did its recognition that the political partition was an established fact.'[1] Towards the end of 1927, in a letter to Pamela Travers, AE mentions that he may have to go to the United States ' to see if our American friends will continue to pay up. If not, the paper will end next year.' In the midst of all this, the *Irish Statesman* suddenly found

[1] *New York Times*, 13th April, 1930.

itself threatened with ruinous legal proceedings, the authors of a collection of Irish folk-songs having decided that the only answer to a caustic criticism in the *Statesman* of their work was a libel action.

The need of additional financial assistance was now imperative, and on 14th January, 1928, AE sailed for New York. His mission seemed to his Dublin circle a great adventure for him, and the occasion was celebrated by Oliver Gogarty in a Miltonic sonnet :

> Dublin transmits you, famous, to the West.
> America shall welcome you, and we,
> Reflected in that mighty glass, shall see,
> In full proportion, power at which we guessed,
> Who live too near the eagle and the nest
> To know the pinion's wild supremacy :
> But yours, of all the wings that crossed the sea,
> Carries the wisest heart and gentlest.
> It is not multitudes, but man's idea
> Makes a place famous. Though you now digress,
> Remember to return, as, back from Rome,
> Du Bellay journeyed to his Lyré home ;
> And Plutarch, willingly, to Chaeronea
> Returned, and stayed, lest the poor town be less.

The 'heaven-assailing architecture' of New York and Chicago was to become a fairly familiar sight to AE during the years which remained to him, a considerable part of which was to be taken

A Memoir of AE

up with visits to America. He lectured far and wide through the States, discovering in himself an acceptability to large audiences, and a facility in addressing them, which pleased and surprised himself. His kindly and picturesque presence, the attractive combination in him of an almost boyish capacity for admiration with the modest self-assurance of the man who has been ' thoroughly faithful to himself', won him favour wherever he went. And of all the United States' distinguished visitors, AE's impressions were of a kind likely to please his eager and generous hosts. He was reminded by the wonders of American architecture, not of any ' mushroom growth ', but of antiquity, the youth of the world—of Nineveh and Babylon. ' Architecture is the great contemporary American art. The railway-stations, even, are awe-inspiring. Entering the Grand Central or Pennsylvania stations, one almost feels the head should be bared and speech in a whisper, so like do they seem in their vastness to temples of the mysteries but for the crowds which hurry about at their secular business.'

Ernest Boyd kindly contributes the following :

' I dined with him on January 27, at the house of the eminent lawyer and friend of Horace

A Memoir of AE

Plunkett's, James Byrne. It was a most remarkable triumph for AEtheism, because, after dinner, puffing his old pipe, AE sat in the drawing-room and talked, while some twenty men sat spell-bound. The group included the outstanding lights of the Bar, a General, all the leading editors of any intellectual pretensions in the country, Wilson's right-hand man, Colonel House, and a sprinkling of millionaire Irish-American industrialists. It was a far cry from the simplicities of 17 Rathgar Avenue, but AE talked as if Violet might bring in tea and cake at any moment. It was the finest and most unspoiled picture I have of AE in America.

'For the rest, on that occasion (his first visit) I had several long talks alone with him, in which his lost hopes for Ireland were evident—his praise of America ardent but, I thought, far-fetched and uncritical. For example, he even argued seriously—and this not for the flattery of lecture audiences—that American girls were created beautiful to goad men on to endeavours without which the United States could not develop.

'On that first visit also arrangements were made, in order to help him personally, that he

AE IN AMERICA

should lecture for six months at Yale. When all the necessary wires had been pulled, AE declined the offer, much to the disgust of James Byrne and others, who wanted to help Plunkett's famous lieutenant. Of AE as a lecturer I can vouch for his hold upon audiences, mostly very vaguely informed as to his ideas. I once presided at a lecture which he gave at Columbia University and was struck by one thing—his verbal memory of his own words, for while he was speaking I could hear him saying word for word the same things to me as far back as 1913. Although he held a battered manuscript in his hand, I did not see him once refer to it.'

He had particular reason to be pleased by his audiences' interest in Ireland, especially when, abandoning his economic subject, he told the tale of Irish literature, the unveiling of the heroic past by Standish O'Grady, the arrival of Yeats, and the crowd of poets of whom he himself appeared to be the venerable and prolific father. He saw a good deal of American life, even of its pleasures, and he looked on with some disapproval at the light lovemaking that went on under his eyes. 'In America love has been made so easy that there is no love-poetry I can read', he wrote to Miss Willy Denijs, quoting a poem of his own suggested to him by his observations:

> They stilled the sweetest breath of song
> Who loosed from love its chains,
> Who made it easy to be borne,
> A thing that had no pains.
>
> A dusk has blighted Psyche's wings,
> And its wild beauty dies:
> The fragrance and the glow were born
> Of its own agonies.

The lecturing tour was a great success, and returning to Ireland at the end of March he brought with him a sum of money large enough to carry the *Irish Statesman* through its immediate difficulties.

The article in which he summed up the impressions of his visit was quoted and widely read in the United States. He had attracted public attention there; and he was hardly back in Dublin when an invitation arrived from Yale University to attend there in the summer to have a degree conferred on him. It seemed to him a compliment to Irish literature which he should accept, and no doubt the prospect of renewed excitement and acclaim was not unpleasing to him. So, instead of taking his usual holiday in Donegal he set off once more across the Atlantic in June.

A Memoir of AE

Unfortunately I have no record of his adventures on this trip, or of the distinguished friends he must have made. The only literary relic of it is the little poem on the waves of the mid-Atlantic (he was an excellent sailor),

> How lonely and lovely those valleys.

22

During the autumn the great subject of discussion in Ireland was the Censorship Bill, and the natural arena for debate among the intellectuals was the *Irish Statesman*. There were good brains on both sides, and opponents of the Bill—including Shaw, Yeats, AE and even Catholic writers like Padraic Colum—did not have the argument all their own way: Shaw, in particular, doing no good to his cause by his boisterous over-statement. The truth was that, in the opinion of a good many people of all parties and religious persuasions, the Free State Government, if it should succeed in stemming the influx of 'corrupt literature', would have gone far towards justifying all the recent revolutionary changes. The effectiveness of the measure was the practical question, and it was of course extremely doubtful that the Bill could arrest that private propaganda with regard to which all the nations of the world appear to be defenceless. But the part of the Bill which concerned Irish writers, and brought them out almost in a body against it, was the clause in which the denunciation of any literature 'calculated to excite sensual passion' was permitted, without, as AE said, any qualification of its being evil or criminal or indecent. His anger made him both lucid and eloquent, and in articles (much admired by Shaw and George Moore) he defended what he conceived to be the cause not only of the rights of literature but of civil liberty, with Miltonic spirit. He protested particularly against what seemed a threat to intellectual liberty in the inclusion of books 'tending to inculcate principles contrary to public morality'. Was there to be an enforced orthodoxy of thought? An incident in Galway, where a group of fanatics, breaking into a library, had taken out books by Shaw, Maeterlinck, Turgenev and others, and publicly burned them, 'without any action we have heard of being taken to punish them', appeared to be an omen of what might happen.

As things have turned out, the powers given by the Bill have been used with moderation, only

A Memoir of AE

such publications as in the view of the Censors offended the laws of decency having so far been banned; and AE's fears of a threat to intellectual freedom have proved groundless. Literature, it may be said, has no real quarrel with puritanism, which can give a very good account of itself in literature: English literature had in fact to come to terms with puritanism. And in Ireland, was it not for a literature meriting the name of 'national' to come to some kind of terms with Irish Catholic puritanism? The censorship has not so far sensibly altered the character of Irish literature, though it has borne somewhat hardly on certain conscientious Irish novelists by depriving them of their sales in Ireland. One immediate result was to give an impetus to Yeats's project of an Irish Academy of Letters, to which, as will be seen, when the *Irish Statesman* had been discontinued, AE was to devote some of his energies. But a certain weariness and disillusionment began in AE at this time, and is freely expressed in his letters. The Ireland he now felt about him was not the Ireland of his earlier dreams and prophesyings. Irish literature, in particular, seemed to shrink within narrower bounds, and was no longer the spiritual manifestation of a National Being, which had its origins in Ireland's heroic

A Memoir of AE

past and comprehended all writers of Irish birth who had caught from it their flame.

Of the libel action, which came on in October–November 1928, Professor Osborn Bergin kindly sends the following note :

> 'I have not read O'Sullivan's review since the time of its appearance, but I remember that it struck me as both severe and well merited. The book [*i.e.* the "Song-Book" criticised] is full of shocking inaccuracies. As AE said in evidence, it seemed to him the reaction of a scholar to slovenly work, or words to that effect. For my part I was not particularly startled by the review, because I was familiar with the way scholars write about each other and about the unscholarly, *e.g.* Stokes in *Revue Celtique* : " such stuff seems to me the drivel of a besotted charlatan ". But AE might have been more cautious about printing it if his mind had not been occupied with preparations for his first American visit, which was arranged before there was any thought of review or libel action. The whole case gave huge delight to a large audience, and great satisfaction to the lawyers (as it cost hundreds of pounds a day) and I should think misery and boredom to the un-

fortunate jurors, who got 5s. each for a week's loss of business, and from beginning to end understood hardly a word of the arguments. In the end they brought in an inconclusive verdict, as they could not decide whether there was libel or not (after listening to an exposition on the law of libel for more than two hours, a time of joy to the judge—he gave only one Latin quotation, but the rest of his discourse might as well have been in Greek). The plaintiffs were ill-advised to appeal, for the appeal was dismissed without calling on the defence, and merely added another item to their bill.'

The defendants' costs in the trial were about £2500, and part of this amount was raised by the editor's admirers, in response to an appeal signed by a number of distinguished people, including Lord Lansdowne. More money might have been obtained from America, so long as AE remained editor, and the paper have been continued indefinitely, but he had begun to wish for freedom. He had been writing editorial articles almost continually since 1905, and was showing signs of fatigue. Moreover, there were one or two books which he wanted to write, and at odd moments he had begun *The Avatars*. It is doubtful, however, whether

A Memoir of AE

AE's main talent as a prose-writer was not best exercised in his journalism—a word which has acquired a somewhat invidious distinction from literature, chiefly because modern journalism has for the most part annexed the whole genial province of occasional writing. The 'essay' in particular has become the 'article'. And yet the examples of Ben Jonson and Landor are enough to show that a resolute intention to write nothing but literature does not secure the most careful writing from the inattention of posterity. The writer who would be named by most critics as the master of English prose at its best is Swift, and in Swift there is much of what would now be called journalism. Indeed, why should not Goethe's saying that all true poetry is 'occasional' be extended to prose literature? One is even inclined sometimes to wonder whether a vital part of recorded human utterance has not been lost in the waste of ephemeral publications. And it is certainly true that men of great character and force have achieved in their nation, through the conduct of famous journals, an influence and authority comparable to that exercised by literary dictators like Dr. Johnson over their little circle. If this applies generally to famous editors, it has a particular application to AE, for during the seven years of the *Irish States-*

A Memoir of AE

man he had gone a good way towards creating in Ireland that 'public opinion' which Lecky had declared to be Ireland's great desideratum. It was a new thing in Ireland for cultivated people to be provided with an organ of literary and cultural opinion of the standard of the great London weeklies; and that they had it was entirely due to the inexhaustible energies and versatile talents of AE. It was, then, this public adviser in cultural matters — 'litterarum existimatorem justum' — whom Dublin University decided to honour when, in the summer of 1929, it conferred on him the degree of Doctor of Letters. The Public Orator expressed the claims of the poet-economist in ingenious Latin :

> 'Salutamus civem patriae amantissimum, qui agricolas nostros operas mutuas ita dare reddere docuit ut dum unusquisque alterius commodis inservire videretur ipse ditior et felicior fieret ; qui vatis, inquam, afflatum divinum cum negotiorum cottidianorum usu (res prius dissociabiles) egregio temperamento miscuit.'

John Galsworthy stood beside AE to receive the same distinction, and at the festivities following, AE pleased the company with a humorous and witty speech.

A Memoir of AE

A step towards the recovery of the Lane Pictures seemed to have been taken this year when the Dublin City Commissioners procured Charlemont House for a collection of modern pictures; thus redeeming a pledge given many years previously that, as Sir Hugh Lane was known to have stipulated, a gallery would be provided for his gift. This was a cause dear to AE, and once more he called upon the British authorities, whose last argument he declared had now gone, to act 'like gentlemen'.

There was a sale of AE's own pictures in New York in October 1929, at prices much above his usual modest Dublin charge, several of them being priced at $500 each. The sale was disappointing, but it produced a sum useful in view of the approaching loss of his regular income.

Many letters reached him on the announcement in the issue of 12th April, 1930, that the *Irish Statesman* would no longer appear. One from Yeats praises the 'dignity and grace' of the editor's Farewell, which is as follows:

> 'For twenty-five years the Editor has been a weekly commentator in the *Irish Homestead* and in the *Irish Statesman* on politics, literature and the arts, and he could not have continued much longer, nor would it have been right for him to

A Memoir of AE

have continued. He belongs to a movement which began at the latter end of last century and which has by now almost spent its force. A new Ireland is growing up with its own ideals of a culture, a social order and a civilisation. It is only right that those who belong to the new era should be its propagandists, and not elderly men whose minds have lost flexibility and who have come to a kind of spiritual deafness when they listen to the talk of young genius. Before that last infirmity weighs more heavily upon the Editor, he feels it is best to cease criticism and comment. He can still, like George Herbert, " relish versing " and on looking back he finds his greatest pleasure was the discovery of Irish talent. He hopes that his part in many controversies will be forgotten. But he would like to be remembered for this, that he was the friend of the Irish poets, those who make the soul of the nation.'

23

AE was always a warrior, but not of that ' happy ' kind whose life is wrought upon the plan that pleased their boyish thought. On the contrary, as I have already had occasion to remark, his life is

A Memoir of AE

an example of the way in which Destiny often decides not only what is best for us, but what we ourselves really like best. He tells Professor Gaus of Wisconsin of his 'hope to start writing books I have long wanted to write, but could not find time or energy to undertake while I was an editor'; but he was not one of those men—any more than was Socrates or Dr. Johnson—whose minds work best in solitude, and his most fruitful meditations were caught from contact with other minds. What he liked best in life was talk. And Destiny now contrived for him the most strenuous and variegated experience of his life, and one, as it proved, not uncongenial to him, a long and elaborately organised lecturing-tour in America. AE had not Yeats's natural instinct for the platform, but some kind of audience was necessary to him, and he had already proved that he could hold large audiences. Adventures to the brave! AE was not only brave but dauntless. Early in May 1930, Harvard University offered him a degree, to be conferred on him at the Summer Commencement, but as he had already arranged to go to the States in the autumn, he did not make the special journey. The plan for the 'George Russell (AE) Lecturing Tour' is a formidable document. He was to lecture everywhere at the Agricultural

A Memoir of AE

Colleges and Universities on the philosophy of the
'National Being', and the tour was to be in
furtherance of a scheme for the organisation of
'Citizen Councils'. In September he set off.

In a series of letters to Joseph O'Neill he gives a
lively account of his adventures, interspersed with
some reflections on Irish matters.

'GRAND FOREST, DAKOTA
'13/10/30

'Here I am well on my way to California.
I had a hectic week in New York. I was movie-
toned talking with Al Smith, later with Dr.
Murray Butler of Columbia, was radioed over
the United States in a twenty-minutes speech.
Two days after I went into a news-reel theatre
and heard myself talk to Dr. Butler and came out
thinking I was clever to talk like that. I came
to Chicago and talked to the Agricultural
Branch of Chamber of Commerce and lectured
to the Drama League, went on to Madison,
where there was a great agricultural conference
at the University. Made two speeches, talked
to a girls' literary society, and was radioed again
over the States. I found myself popular. I
was told that Wilbur, one of Hoover's cabinet,

had a meeting at same time as mine and his was half empty, the folk flocking to hear me, so that I had to be relayed to another hall; then I went on to St. Paul, Minneapolis, talked at University and preached an hour sermon at the theatre on Sunday which was radioed over the United States. The Sermon was on the building up of a rural civilisation. I talked to the Saturday Club, and made a second speech at the University on the Irish literary movement and then came on here, where I talked in the State College in the morning, and attend a civic dinner of the town in my honour to-night. So you can see I am kept busy. I travel by night and speak by day. I am off after the dinner to St. Paul again to speak at some agricultural settlement. I am becoming fluent and brazen and in the midst of it all am pining to be back in Ireland. It is a devil of a long tour, from now to next March. I am to meet tomorrow the New Great American novelist Rolvaag, who wrote *Giants in the Earth*. I am a quarter through his book, which I think good and well imagined. Of course he is a Norwegian. I thought of you here during an hour before I go to that civic dinner and felt I must write to some one in Ireland and keep myself in touch with that little island. I saw Diarmuid [his son] in Chicago and found him well, becoming Americanised. He said " Yep " to my remarks. He was quite pleased to see me. I was also in Washington for some hours and admired the way in which when you see a minister a photographer appears mysteriously and photos you and the minister. The art of advertising is burnished here to fullest efficiency. I share in it. There is hardly anything public men do here which is not photographed, or movie-toned. When Al Smith came to be movie-toned with me he switched on an electric smile of welcome and shook my hand as if he was my blood-brother. Then, for he is a human being, he whispered me " I did this for four months during the Presidential contest ". The photographers tell ministers what to do. The Secretary of Agriculture in Washington was told by the photographer to hold some papers and to appear to be explaining them to me. He obeyed instantly. It is an amazing country, but the people are the kindest under heaven and are like great lovable children for the most part. Of course, there are very fine and subtle minds among them too. Is there anything happening in Ireland ? The size of this country is appalling.

A Memoir of AE

You start on a ride and the fields go away to infinity and the sense of vastness is impressive. The western folk are very eager and energetic and full of hope and imaginations about their country. Their power of organisation is stupendous. I was over the Land of Lakes Creamery headquarters in St. Paul, a federation of 400 creameries, and the way they did their business was marvellous. If Patrick Hogan saw that huge place it would give him ideas about Irish dairying. They fill me with envy, so monstrously efficient are they. I must now prepare for my civic dinner.'

'PALACE HOTEL, SAN FRANCISCO
'12/11/30

'Here I am after gazing on the Pacific with a wild surmise, writing from a hotel in San Francisco. Lord, what a heap of travelling I have done and more talking than I have ever done in my life. I have three times radioed my ideas over the whole United States, and five times over local areas. The last time was at Seattle, where I was the guest of the Chamber of Commerce at lunch and talked to five hundred American business men and was radioed at the same time. It is awful feeling you are talking to

A Memoir of AE

an invisible as well as to a visible audience. I talked to the Chicago Chamber of Commerce when I was there. I laugh when I think I, a mystic poet, can impress the hard-faced American business man. I will have this kind of work until the end of March next, speaking at Universities and other gatherings. I am supposed to be working up interest for the creation of an Agricultural Foundation in the States. The scenery in the Rockies is magnificent. I saw all the scenery of the wild-west stories, the deserts with sage-bushes mottling them and snow mountains, vast beyond imagination, and monstrous valleys inconceivable in the long leagues they stretch and more mountains, canyons, dizzy deeps with rivers. I moved for a week or ten days amid mountainy country on both the east and west side of the Rockies. I like this side of the States. The people are natural and kind, and one meets extraordinarily nice and cultivated folk. I was amused to find a little community created fifteen years before because Daniel Wallace read an article of mine on the rural community and bought land and started his village on it. There it is, a church (not my idea), a bank, and a score of comfortable farms and houses, and he told me I was responsible.

A Memoir of AE

It did not pan out as he wanted it. But it flourished all the same. I get no news of Ireland in the papers, I only gathered that there was some kind of row on Armistice Day. San Francisco is an amazing city, all gold, blue and rose electric lights. At a distance coming over the waters it appears like a faery metropolis built of diamonds, topaz and rubies. When you get closer you find these flashing jewels appeal to you to buy some brand of cigarettes or to go and see somebody acting. But at a distance the effect is better than Aladdin's garden of jewels. I will be here for four days, then I go to Los Angeles the rival city, and after that to Arizona. Doesn't the name recall to you your Zane Grey and other masters of American fiction? Then I go to Texas and work my way back to New York by 19th December, when I have a week's rest before I start my second three months. It is warm here in November as summer at home. But a week ago I was in Northern States where the winter had already set in. The hugeness of this country is most impressive, and curiously even these Western States, some of which were only opened fifty years ago, seem already old settlements. It is because the farms and houses are well built and attractive and the roads everywhere broad and well-laid that the new country even seems to have centuries behind it. In Seattle, a huge city with enormous sky-scrapers and about 500,000 people, I was pointed out a middle-aged man who was the first man born in the city. Yet Seattle is larger than Dublin and fifty times as busy. The whole of America seems to be inspired by Longfellow's line

 Let us then be up and doing.

I wish he had written with equal persuasiveness " Let us then lie down and idle", and I would have enjoyed my journey more. I am hypnotised myself to be up and doing. I would like to go into a hermitage for six months when I get back. Lord, how I wish it was over, and I have only done one quarter of my engagements. I feel Ireland lies away beyond the horizon a remote memory, so much of a whirlwind has carried me about. I am a leaf blown by the wind but a leaf which has to rustle loudly as it rolls. I hope you and Mrs. O'Neill are well. I am keeping in good health in spite of my hard work. I would have died in Ireland if I had had to do what I do here. It is the electricity in the air which makes everybody active and makes them old before their time. I get a sense of solid well-meaning goodness and public spirit in the people and great competence in organising whatever they do. It will be the great State of the world for centuries and it will probably be deeper and better after an economic setback, which I think is coming on it because the industrial and agricultural sides of the nation have so perfected themselves that fewer and fewer people can do the work. Hence the rural exodus here and the unemployment in the cities.'

'Santa Barbara, Biltmore
'19/11/30

'Bless you for your letter. Here I am in a Spanish civilisation that is surrounded by the lovely Spanish architecture. It is warm here in winter. Too hot for me though the folk here think it cool. Palmtrees and roses and flowers blooming, oranges on trees, and lemons, a place for millionaires with rich gardens and houses and nothing to do except to play games, make love, and do all the idle things the wealthy find to do. I lectured last night to a select club of rich folk, who put me up in a palace of a hotel, and placed motor-cars at my service, and generally were kind. But what a place to rot one's faculties in by its sheer beauty, sea, sunshine, palms, eucalyptuses, gardens, palaces in the Spanish fashion, lovely hills, purple and shining. I am just off to San Diego, then back to San Francisco, where I was already. I lectured at the California school of technics where Millikan, the greatest of living physicists, presides, a charming man, a Nobel prizeman for his researches into the atom. I have gained an immense circle of acquaintances in the States. The college and university professors are generally very cultivated and pleasant people. I think I like the Western side of the States better than the Eastern. The Rockies are marvellous and here the Japanese Sea brings summer along the coast like the gulf stream in Ireland, only warmer. You would love this country at first sight and then feel if you did not get out of it you would rot your soul with idleness and beauty. After San Francisco I am off to Arizona, Texas, Virginia, and other states, landing at New York 15th Dec. having finished the first half of my journey. Lord, I will be glad to be back in Dublin again. I wish I could go into a hermitage for a whole month and sit at the mouth of a cave looking into an empty valley and an empty

A Memoir of AE

sky with no human being or noise on earth or in air. Possibly I would get bored after a month, but the first week of silence and stillness, what a delight.'

'(SOUTHERN LINES, PACIFIC)
'29/11/30

'I am writing in the middle of a desert which has lasted since morning and seems to show no signs of ending until night. It is the Californian desert which will shortly blend into the Arizonian desert. I write to tell you that sage and cactus and the things you read of in Wild West stories are real. But I saw no cowboys in the desert. I saw some in Los Angeles, but I suspect they were dressed up for cinema, as I believe all that belongs to a past generation. It is devilish hot though it is November. It is hotter here than our hottest midsummer. I am wondering what Karma brought me in my old age round the world to this continent. Yesterday I addressed seven hundred and fifty business men at lunch in San Francisco and was radioed over the State. This is about the eighth time I have radioed speeches, four times over the whole of the States. If I was a criminal I would not have the ghost of a chance of escap-

A Memoir of AE

ing, as even the negro waiters on the trains know me and ask "Are you AE?" My wife writes me that I was seen talking to Al Smith on the movie-tones in my own city. Lord, what a life. But I will be glad to look back on it. California is the most exciting and beautiful of all the States with mountains, deserts, palms, cactus, orange groves, forests, and a perpetual heat, with Spanish names and the beautiful Spanish architecture still surviving. I think there is more feeling for beauty and poetry here than elsewhere. I spent a day with Jeffers, the Californian poet, a great fellow I think, very grave and noble to look at. His Greek free verse play about "Clytaemnestra" is great stuff, the most savage and intense poetry written in America. The "Roan Stallion" is good and strange also. I am to speak somewhere in Arizona to-morrow and then I go to Texas and I wilt at the thought of the heat before me. Winter has not the same meaning in the low latitudes as in the high. People call it cool when the temperature is near 100. I believe it goes up to 120 in the summer. I see from the train window a desert going on the one side into infinity and on the other to remote pink-coloured mountains. Yet I believe that there are people who get so infatuated with the desert that they won't leave it. I am not of their class. I think you would like this trans-Rocky land for its vastness and romance. I think people here might love and hate mightily, but they are pleasant to meet and endlessly kind and hospitable. I find my poems and *The Candle of Vision* very well known, the latter a kind of bible for many mystics, and the American committee which brought me over are distributing thousands of *The National Being* free in order to work up interest in a rural civilisation. I am supposed to be awaking U.S.A. to the danger of its rural exodus, and they are going I understand to raise funds for an Agricultural Foundation to plan things out so that the States won't be altogether urban. I believe I am having an effect. I have got over my fright addressing great Chambers of Commerce, and start hypnotising square-jawed business men with a relish. They are emotional folk and they like the mingling of poetry and economics I give them. I know you are cursing my handwriting, but it is the rocking of the train over the desert. Anyhow I will shut up now. I write because I do not want to forget Ireland.'

A Memoir of AE

'HOTELS LANIER, EL JARDIN, RALEIGH
' 12/12/30

'I am still in Texas, having returned from Louisiana, the most dilapidated blue-mouldy decrepit state I ever looked at, with the great forest moss dripping from the trees making them look as if they had the mange, with neglected houses unpainted with holes in the roof, and a lazy people infested by the hookworm, making cotton to grow or tending sugar-cane. The Great Mississippi wanders sleepily through it and the forests seem to rise out of swamps. I suppose it is the best example of what the Southern defeat in the Civil War did to the South. Texas is a more lively state made prosperous by oil, but not very interesting from the painter's point of view, not like magical Arizona with its rose-amethyst mountains and its cactus-covered deserts where a man might live and meditate happily if he had no concern about rattlesnakes. I have no doubt the engineering genius of the American people will irrigate this waste land and turn a perfectly good desert into homesteads giving oranges, grape-fruit, peaches and nuts. I think I would prefer it as desert, though in California irrigation

A Memoir of AE

has made hundreds of miles of orange groves possible and they look beautiful with their golden fruit. I find my ideas about a rural civilisation fit in with much the agricultural reformers are beginning to think, and I talk loftily to Chambers of Commerce or economists at State Universities about their defects economically. But it is all very tiring this continual travel. Yesterday I left Baton Rouge at 3 o.c., trained it all night, got in here at 11 o.c. and talk at the University at 3.30, have a dinner in the evening and more talk ; then to-morrow morning I go another day journey sleeping in train or not sleeping if it jolts as trains sometimes will, even the best-regulated Pullman cars. The folk in the Universities are quite nice people, often very cultivated, and the science side especially is very efficient. They are strong on engineering. Einstein has just come to America and gone to the California Institute of Technology where Millikan, the greatest American scientist, presides, a fine man I think whom I found very friendly. They are going together to make some investigations about some mathematical arcana which I have no doubt will be world-shaking if the world understands what it is all about. It is curious that Eddington, Jeans,

A Memoir of AE

Einstein, Whitney, the greatest American chemist, are all becoming mystics, and I think we are in for an era of mysticism as a reaction from the solid materialistic science of my boyhood. Jeans states his belief in a divine mind like Eddington, and Whitney says all his science is only an educated man's way of stating something which really exists only because we live and move and have our being in infinite deity : it is all very exciting this change, and I would not wonder if the scientists did not lean to the poets for illumination. Santayana begins his last book on Materialism by quoting my poem " The Virgin Mother ". I would not wonder, if the scientists become mystical, if they should elect me as an honorary member of the British Association along with Yeats and other poets with an internal light.'

'New York City
'27/1/31

'I see you are at your usual winter sports. I guess the cold here is as near zero or below it as in your favourite Alps. But it is a dry electric cold which stirs and excites the brain. It is the kind of thing that makes the Americans be up and

A Memoir of AE

doing to their undoing. For they have been overdoing production in agriculture and industry, and with fewer people producing more than they or the world can consume they are staring at each other in surprise as they thought if they produced well all would be well and they find they are producing unemployed. I am in New York for three days rest. On Thursday I go to a dinner the Poetry Society of America is giving me and that night I start for Montreal, and I will be away for three months I think, or nearly that, and that ends my Odyssey, and I return to our quiet land; no racket which could be kicked up in Ireland will seem to me noisy after the noise here. But it's a great and likeable country with crowds of fine folk, most loveable people in it. They suggest a yet unblended people, all sorts, Finns, Irish, Swedes, Russians, Germans, etc., continuing their own existence, and habits in a kind of way, half-blended, like icebergs half-melted into the warm water.

I will be dotting off the days now until I get back in April. Ireland here seems remote at times as the pre-war world, and seven thousand miles away like something one heard of about one's cradle very far off and long ago. I daresay you will think it shows how far away I am

A Memoir of AE

that I wonder occasionally if there will be a new literary movement in Ireland chronicling the close of the old era and the re-emergence of the pagan; not my kind of paganism, I fear, but one which will make people regret that they attacked writers like Yeats and myself, and hold us up as models of Christian gentlemen. It seems funny, the Indian Conference with its pompous bestowal of political independence, minus foreign relations, minus financial control and minus military control. It is as if I was your guardian and said to you, "Joe, my boy, you are come to manhood and independence. But for safety I will keep your money under my control, and it is better that I should have a veto on your friends and I think it best to have a policeman to look after you. Except for this, Joe, my boy, you are a free man." It sounds like that from a distance. I wonder what it sounds like in India. I will read with interest what Gandhi says. I wonder is he a clever man! His economics are infantile.

'You must come here some time and see the sky-scrapers. They are immense and loftily beautiful in the light. The great Empire Building is like a tower of pearl in the sunny air, a tower of pearl about seven or eight hundred feet high. I must close up now and go to bed. I am tired after an idle day. Resting in a chair makes one sleepy.

'Somebody sent me a description of my oratory. My hair is black! I cast spells. I have to. It is the only way I can overcome my audiences.'

'CHICAGO
'14/2/31

'Here I am just arrived from Detroit, one of those gigantic new cities built largely round Henry Ford's enterprise, but with huge skyscrapers like all the big American cities, making you dizzy and awed when you look up at them. I have come here for a conference with some agriculturally interested folk who want to start an agricultural foundation to save American agriculture on my lines. I think they are a great deal too ambitious. They want to raise five million dollars. I don't know where I go after that. My schedule comes to-morrow from New York. I have been doing some wild travelling during the past ten days. I lectured at Lansing February 6th, left it same day and lectured at Grand Rapids, went to Detroit on 7th and lectured there. Then on 8th went to Wooster

University and did my turn. Left Wooster and went to Buffalo, stayed there a night and went to Ithaca, where I lectured at Cornell University 12th, talked again next night and after that took a night-train at 12 o.c. for Detroit where I lectured on 13th and again on 14th and arrived here to-night, rushing off after lecture to train. It is the hell of a life. But I am standing up against it very well and I hope by the grace of God to wind up all my business here at the end of April and start home at the beginning of May. I was in Montreal in Canada before I went to Lansing. I liked Montreal where I talked twice and found delightful folk. The world was white for thousands of miles and the temperature below zero, which makes one's blood tingle. It is a dry electric cold not like our damp cold. But, oh Lord, won't I luxuriate in idleness when I get back and rise up in the morning with the heavenly feeling that there are no trains to catch or speeches to make. I have become the expert lecturer by practice and face my audiences without turning a hair, I who used to be terrified at speaking a word before a crowd. The restless unceasing energy of these people is amazing. They are heaping up economic dangers for their own civilisation by over-energy resulting in overproduction. Fewer and fewer people are required to do the work, science and mergers and rationalisation and more efficient machinery creating unemployment. The country is filled with relief schemes. Every state and city has them. I guess there must be about six million unemployed or five million at the very least. They try to minimise it. I think there is going to be tribulation in this great country and that it will deepen national life. They are big enough to pull through. But it will be a pull. I hear nothing of Ireland in the papers. We are not murderous enough to interest the cable companies, and there is no sign anywhere of the former disposition to magnify our importance. It will take me some time to make up past history when I get back. Seven months of Irish life and I not knowing about anything! I who used to keep track of all that went on. I fear the censors are active. Somebody told me that at first their activities were a genuinely important guide to immoral literature, but that now they have taken to censoring books in which it is a sort of puzzle to find the temptation. I would have had great fun commenting on the censors if the *Irish Statesman* was still in being. Do you miss it? Does anybody?

A Memoir of AE

or is it forgotten and gone behind time like Griffith's *Sinn Fein* and the *United Irishman*?'

'NEW YORK
'12/3/31

'I found your letter when I arrived here this evening. I will be able to tell you endless things about American Universities and colleges. Tomorrow I am to instruct the teachers in training here upon rural economics. They also gather the state agricultural officials. I found that my *National Being*, the rural part of it, is well known everywhere. I think about ten thousand copies of it have been distributed through U.S.A. and I was told that the Harvard professor of Rural Sociology said I was the only writer on the subject with any creative imagination. They are very depressed here about both agriculture and urban industry, and listen eagerly to any solution of their problems. They are trying to start a rural foundation to organise the farmers on old-world lines, and that is one result of my lectures. I feel as if I had really started some kind of thinking but I am terrified at the scale they think of working on. They want five million dollars! I have been all through the Southern States,

A Memoir of AE

Georgia, Alabama, Virginia, North and South Carolina, and I feel very much at home in the South. They had a rural civilisation founded of course on slave labour before the civil war. It went to pieces after the slaves were freed. But there are everywhere beautiful houses, colonial architecture it is called, lovely houses with great white Corinthian pillars all about them. They give the sensation of great beauty, often with magnificent gardens. I was over one of these gardens a week ago, a place outside Charleston. It looked like the gardens of a great king, artificial lakes, mighty oaks, terraces, flowers, alleys of trees, magnolias, azaleas. It was designed by French landscape gardeners about two hundred years ago and built by slave labour. There are great numbers of rich places, some going to ruin, others are bought up by the Northern inhabitants and kept in good order. The Northern victor inherits the civilisation of the Southern rural aristocracy. I understand the Confederate point of view now as I never did before, and I rather like the Southern passion for a rural life and culture as against the machine civilisation of the New England industrialists. They are such nice human beings these Southern folk.

A Memoir of AE

'By the time you get this I will have only one month more in U.S.A. My last engagement is I think 29th April. It will probably take a week or ten days more to wind up my affairs in New York, get a ship, etc., and some time in May I should be knocking at your door.'

24

Vale and other Poems appeared while he was in America—an impressive little book, giving utterance to the profound spiritual longings which kept the soul of this untiring man detached and solitary amid all the distractions described in the foregoing letters, with their little touches of vanity. The prevalent mood of these poems is one of sombre brooding over the memory of those who through death or the vicissitudes of life are no longer direct objects of love, and they reveal a soul which must have been a prey to changing affections. He asks the familiar questions: in one of the most touching of the poems, thinking of the friends of his early life—how will he know them again when they are no longer as he remembers them? in another, is new love a treachery to the old? And he consoles himself with a philosophy not unlike that of

A Memoir of AE

Epipsychidion. But he writes lightly of the poems to Pamela Travers :

'I see my *Vale* has been reprinted. As one goes down hill one automatically collects prestige as a snowball gathers snow. I suppose when I am half senile my repute for wisdom will be at its height. "What a wise old bird", people will say. But I was only wise when I was about twenty-one or thereabouts—all evolution is by way of loss, as Bateson the anthropologist said. You lose some characters, and change from a white intensity to a many-coloured dullness.'

There is truth in this as a criticism of his poems. The later poetry does not breathe the glowing conviction of *Homeward* : yet through his ceaseless interest in all verse, and lifelong practice, he has acquired mastery in his particular craft.

He returned to Ireland in May 1931, spending a few days in London, where he called on his old friend George Moore. ' He began at once about American architecture ', said Moore, telling of the visit, ' and went on for about twenty minutes, until at last I said, " And now, Russell, shall we have a little chat ? " ' Another London friend noticed

A Memoir of AE

a change in him : he had become an entertaining talker, an anecdotist ; he could even talk of wine and food, and he seemed to have been as pleasingly diverted in America as Erasmus was in England by the enthusiastic kisses of female adorers. It was hard to recognise the old AE in this lion of American dinner-parties. But the truth probably was that AE had wished to convince himself that he could do this kind of thing as well as everything else, and he soon reverted to his simple habits.

In June he is writing to the American poet, Vachel Lindsay :

> ' I am staying in a remote mountainy district in Donegal. Before the cottage door I see this [*Sketch*. He often thus adorned his letters.] The mountain is Muckish, one of the twelve sacred mountains in Ireland. . . . I amuse myself painting. I had eight months in your country, and feel empty after talking all the time, and came here to fill the empty psyche. Why were you not born here ? You would have upset all our old traditions over which we have brooded too long. I see nobody. I read nothing. I eat griddle bread, drink buttermilk, sit by a turf fire, and walk over hills and sands, and try to empty my mind so that Mother Earth

may come into it and talk to me a little. She
used to breathe in me, and I have hopes she
may sing a little song through me again.'

While in Donegal he had begun a story which he
had long had in mind, *The Avatars*, but could not
get on with it. He had no doubt overworked himself, and he complained of headaches whenever
he tried to write. A little later he is with Yeats
at Coole Park, talking over the proposed Irish
Academy of Letters; and Yeats, as he was going
to America, was glad to leave the task of drawing
up the rules and constitution, registration, etc.,
in his friend's more capable hands. Probably
Russell was not unwilling to take on himself the
business part of the project as a distraction from
domestic trouble, for towards the end of this year
his wife had fallen ill with a serious internal com-
plaint. There was a painful operation, and he
spent several hours with her each day in her room
at the hospital; seeking relief at home from his
depression (as he tells his friend C. M. Grieve,
'Hugh McDiarmid') by writing his little prose
work *Song and its Fountains*. It happened that
Gandhi was in England, and wished to see the
author of *The National Being*, but AE had to
write that he could not go to London owing to his

A Memoir of AE

wife's illness; whereupon Miss Slade, Gandhi's secretary, wired to him, 'Come at once'. 'I did not answer that', said AE afterwards; 'what sort of a woman could she be who expected me to leave a sick wife?' His wife lingered on till 13th February 1932, when she died; and it appears from a letter to Seán O'Faoláin that Russell immediately afterwards went away to London for a while, 'to be alone'. Violet Russell was a remarkable woman, endowed with charm and fortitude. 'She could endure suffering', her husband wrote, 'better than any I have known.' She had early reconciled herself to being the wife of a man of genius, with many avocations and with little taste for domesticity; and was indeed a saint of Theosophy, acknowledging in Karma and Reincarnation the laws of life.

Miss Edith Sitwell described *Song and its Fountains*, which appeared just after Mrs. Russell's death, as 'a mysteriously beautiful book', and indeed it is a beautifully composed little work and in its way unique. Perhaps the nearest thing to it is Traherne's *Centuries of Meditations*, so far as the latter work supplies a commentary on its author's poems. AE's prose pours on impetuously, just like his talk, from which one carried the glow and impetus of his earnest speech, though

A Memoir of AE

often without having received any particular illumination on the subject of his discourse—unless indeed the subject happened to be a practical one. Similarly, from this little book one hardly gains any new understanding of the miracle by which a poem—or for the matter of that, any happy or fruitful idea—comes into being. AE in fact reverses the part of those interpreters summoned in former times by perplexed tyrants to expound their dreams, for it is by his dreams that AE expounds his poetry : and this, as a general explanation of poetry, is to explain that of which we know something by that of which we may think as we please. *Song and its Fountains*, nevertheless, is invaluable as a commentary on AE's own poems, and almost a necessary companion volume to them. In a letter to 'Hugh McDiarmid' he describes the circumstances of its composition, and how he had decided to write only of himself.

'I am very conscious of its imperfections. I wrote it during the long illness of my wife, and I was so distracted that even the proofs were badly corrected and the book has many misprints. I considered the idea of using the confessions of other poets, as for example what Goethe says to Eckermann about verses welling up from the subconscious, but I had not his mood or the moods of other poets under the precise vision one has of one's own consciousness, and decided to speak only of what I could write about with personal knowledge. We have really nothing to write about truly except ourselves. I use the word "ourselves" to include the conscious personality and that vast ocean of life which envelops us, and in which we find our most intimate understanding of the minds of others.'

AE was now a lonely man, and he must have felt the change especially on Sunday evenings, when for many years, week after week, his room had been crowded with eager and varied assemblies, brought thither by curiosity or devotion, as if to share in the mysteries of that sacred abstraction, Ireland. His wife had been an important though unobtrusive figure at these gatherings; but even before her death, and his long absences in America, they had begun to be less frequented than formerly. His talk was more than ever in set harangues, of which Mrs. Kingsley Porter has this account:

'He used to say he owed his memory to poverty. Having so few books in youth he unconsciously memorised whatever he read.

A Memoir of AE

This ability tended to set his conversation into subjects. The type once laid down, ever afterwards the words (which fortunately were always the right ones) kept their same positions. But his repertoire was so great and the moment itself created always so much new talk, he seldom repeated these fixed topics unless you asked him to tell again a certain experience or a certain story.'

From one cause or another, many of the more notable members of his earlier circle had dropped out, and it was no longer to AE that the younger men were turning when, in March of this year, the Cosgrave government came to an end and De Valera at length obtained control. 'I am a lonely man', he writes to Van Wyck Brooks, 'living by myself with a kind maid to look after me, and I sink into reverie and am the more disinclined to comment on public affairs because I am not in much sympathy with the young men who are managing Irish affairs. I do not indeed understand them.' And to Pamela Travers (28th April, 1932):

'I will not be in Donegal until July, and I am going, not to Janie this year, but to Kingsley Porter at Glenveagh, which is about fifteen miles away, remote from everything except mountains and lakes, with not even a village of ten houses nearer than four miles, I think. I wish I could go in June to escape from the flood of piety which will be at high tide at the Eucharistic Congress. I would like at times to fly from Dublin, even from Ireland, so much do I dislike the new generation of bigoted Catholics and political louts who are dominant. Indeed I would go, only for the love I have for the Earth here, and find some village in Cornwall like Stephen MacKenna, and leave all the past behind me. Ireland as a nation I have no further interest in. Indeed I have no interest in nations at all. I feel I belong to a spiritual clan whose members are scattered over the world, and these are my kinsmen, and I would sacrifice any nation, my own quite readily, to promote the interests of that spiritual clan. I once wrote

> We are less children of this clime
> Than of some nation yet unborn,
> Or Empire in the womb of Time,

and this mood of futurism has grown in me until I almost hate the present.'

Yet, however estranged from Irish politics, he still had the poets and writers on his side, and was fond of taunting De Valera's party with its failure

A Memoir of AE

to produce a poet. The writers of the new generation, like those of the earlier, had gathered round him ; and a task to which he was often called, and which he performed most gracefully, was that of introducing new writers, and especially poets, to the public. He now gave a good deal of his attention to the formation of the new Irish Academy of Letters, a body of which he seems to have thought less as an ornamental institution than as an organisation which might be active in defence of the liberties and interests of art and literature. A letter of 10th October, 1932, to Van Wyck Brooks makes this clear:

> 'In Ireland we have a national apathy about literature which I fancy is worse than anything in the States. It began to descend on us after we became self-governing ; before that we were imaginative dreamers. The actual work of self-government tended to make us materialistic, and our papers give not the slightest thought to literature and the arts. A bad censorship completes the depression. As a means of awakening interest again in the spiritual side of nationality we have just formed an Irish Academy of Letters, for which I drew up the rules. The idea of the Academy was Yeats's. We hope to draw attention to young writers of merit by a money-prize

or medal given by their elders in literature, and in other ways to promote the interests of creative literature. We have really all the young men of talent in our association as well as the older famous men like Yeats and Shaw. . . . Shaw altered the rules I drew up by an amendment which Yeats and myself adopted : after December this year nobody will be eligible for election if his election would bring the average age of academicians to be over sixty. Shaw, in spite of his own and of Yeats's vitality, obviously does not contemplate Whitman's " splendid and savage old men ".'

As this was the spirit in which he worked for the Academy it is not altogether surprising that he came into collision with 'orthodoxy', and in January 1933 he writes with glee to St. John Ervine that he has ' had to knock out two Jesuits. I found my old talent for controversy was not altogether rusted, and my last letter aroused a frenzy of vituperation.'

' I exist in Ireland ', he writes to Ervine again in April, ' because it is my duty to leave as many heresies in its literature as possible. The seeds I scatter will come up in the next generation ; indeed, I see a few buds pushing their way up

A Memoir of AE

through the orthodoxies even now. And if I left Ireland, where could I live? I am sixty-seven. If I went to London I know hardly a soul there; I could only read in libraries. Here I have half-a-dozen friends, and we live by our friends not by our country. One's country or one's nation is a brute to be kicked in the ribs. But one's friends are different, one holds to them.'

25

If AE could write as he now did of Irish politics and of the actual Ireland, it was otherwise with the 'Ireland of his dreams', and of this true Ireland he reaffirms in *The Avatars* all his early beliefs and imaginings with unabated conviction. The writing of this story was his chief occupation during 1932–1933. The belief in the coming of a new Avatar was fairly general among Theosophists in the early days; and in the beginning of the century it had been fixed in the mind of Russell by a vivid dream of the birth of a divine Hero in Ireland, which he recorded in a note-book, mentioning that his own child had waked to ask, 'What was the light?' He often spoke of this dream, as if to put it on record, and he remembered it in the Rising of 1916, when

A Memoir of AE

it seemed for a moment—and not only to AE—
that the hour had come for the arrival of an Irish
redeemer. It is necessary to tell all this in order to
show the kind of man Russell really was ; and to
some readers he may seem in this phase to have been
not quite sane, for he had certainly thought of
himself as the prophet of the Avatar : but Ireland
itself at that time was in an exalted mood. The
belief seemed to have faded out somewhat in his
beautiful poem ' Michael ' ; yet now, after all the
glamour had departed and Ireland seemed to have
given up its soul again to dingy politics, it woke in
him again, though it was thought of no longer as
an historic event but with its own truth in the world
of the imagination.

The Avatars is the story of the birth of a new
religion, the religion of the Cosmic Consciousness.
It was part of AE's plan that there should be in
the story no direct appearance of the divine pair
(for the Founders are Aodh and Aoife, a man and
a woman), and that only a rumour of them should
move through its pages ; what is described is the
sense of a new relation to the earth which awakens
in a group of friends—an artist, a philosopher, a
poet, a recluse like Wordsworth's Solitary, and a
few companions—in a rocky solitude in Western
Ireland : the recognition of a divine life in nature.

A Memoir of AE

'I am prodigal of intuitions to-day', exclaims the poet. 'Is there not something different in earth as if it had wakened from long sleep, its soul had come back to its body? And now it has wakened, its body is flushed with magical life. That is not the water of yesterday, nor the air, nor the earth. Some heavenly wine is mixed with the water, and in the air we breathe there is a mingling of the Holy Breath. Earth is living under our feet. It was in a world like this ages ago all the mythologies and fairy tales were born.'

No sayings are reported of the Hero; it is Aoife whose words occasionally drift to our ears, one speech being taken from AE's early pamphlet *The Hero in Man* (a passage, by the way, much admired by George Moore and quoted by him in *Hail and Farewell*). The little community which has begun its existence finds itself suddenly threatened by the State, the monster organisation which has now perfected its mechanism and pounces on any activity not under its control. Its agents arrive suddenly while Aoife is addressing the people, there is a scuffle, and the Avatars mysteriously vanish—whether slain or translated is a kind of theological problem bequeathed to the community in the new religious myth to which they have given birth.

There is beauty, truth and wisdom in the book, but what gives unreality to its characters and to their talk—what almost disqualifies AE as an artist of life—is the extraordinary innocence of his mind. With all his experience of the world he has quite childish notions of it. He is incapable of forming a notion of moral evil, and the only diabolism in the world for him is in the ' State '— ' the State ', as the recluse says, ' is the devil, or rather a multitude of devils '. After the passing of the Avatars, visitors are attracted to the scene of these strange happenings, and it is odd that the chief impersonation of spiritual evil in the tale is a visitor clearly recognisable as George Moore. Those who do not like to think of this passage as an attack on the memory of an old friend explain it as ' dramatic ', but Felim the poet's outburst clearly expresses the feeling of all the characters : ' That thing has worms slinking through its veins, not blood. It would pollute earth to bury him in it. How could you be still while he oozed out that leprosy of imagination ? ' Perhaps in looking back on his own life, Russell found matter for regret in his association with Moore ; perhaps he felt that, partly through Moore, he had not been quite faithful to the heavenly vision; perhaps things said of him by Moore had reached his ears; anyhow, the part played by Moore in his life and in Irish literature suddenly appeared detestable to him, the leer of the outer world, a malign influence instrumental in the frustration of the spiritual hope which had dawned for Ireland. Yet it was not in Russell to feel personal resentment, and if he felt any such inclination he had schooled himself instantly to repress it.

AE's notion of a 'return to nature' is not the ordinary one, nor is his nature-worship that of our modern poetry. No one truly loves nature, we now feel, who does not love it for itself: and we should not only be ready to do without the comforts of life in the wilds but, in the presence of nature, to divest the mind of all its furnishings, its preconceived beliefs and ideas. Indeed it may be said that the love of nature is the consolation of our own agnostic age. The agnostic would probably say that it is the sense of space and mystery, the pure or rarefied air, which give him his exhilaration on the mountain-top, the seashore, or the 'vernal wood'. In Wordsworth, who was of a philosophical turn, the contemplation of nature produced a state which was a wonder to himself and which he made many attempts to describe, though he never quite succeeded in telling what happened within him. But he certainly insisted, as do all the hierophants of nature, that 'impulses' proceeded *from* nature to his own being. In Wordsworth's case, these impulses produced a power of imaginative language in which he far transcended his ordinary level, and a certain courage in proclaiming as truths ideas which on sober reflection he was a little disposed to explain away. In other words, the 'impulse' produced in him an extended range of thought and feeling. And this is probably the normal way in which nature affects us. But if he was not entirely deluded, and if there are such impulses, it is only to be expected that they will quicken each mind according to its faculties. In an artist-poet, for example, it might be expected that the normal visualising faculty would be enhanced by new perceptions from the imagination; and if he should begin to 'see things' in nature—well, I do not see why we should merely point derisively to our foreheads, particularly when he 'the matter can re-word' so well as AE in *The Candle of Vision* and *Song and its Fountains*. Does not Wordsworth himself confess that rather than face an entirely uncommunicative nature he would

> have sight of Proteus rising from the sea,
> or hear old Triton blow his wreathèd horn?

A Memoir of AE

Amongst AE's papers is a letter from Mr. Santayana, who, in *The Realm of Matter*, had quoted the concluding lines of 'The Virgin Mother', perhaps the most explicit assertion of AE's belief in the 'divinity of Earth':

> I look with sudden awe beneath my feet
> As you with erring reverence overhead.

I have the writer's kind permission to quote the letter here.

'Sept. 22, 1933

'DEAR MR. RUSSELL

'It is interesting to know that you have noticed the quotation from your poem, "The Virgin Mother", in my *Realm of Matter*. The devil notoriously quotes scripture for his own purposes, and you must forgive me if I used your words to point a moral which (as I now see) was not the one you intended. The immanence of "love" or potential "beauty" in the material world is, in one sense, a truism. When anything arises or happens we may say that there was a "mysterious" *tendency* in the conditions to produce just that thing. The God of Platonism and Christianity is simply a hypostasis of this tendency in nature towards the good, and is perhaps less "external" than we may think: if the tendency is a distinct power working in things, it is a part of nature. Perhaps this was exactly what you meant by saying that we should reverence earth and not heaven: the real motive force towards the beautiful is inside the world and not beyond.

'The centre of my own interest is at a somewhat different point. I don't know, and I don't much care what the existing motive force is that makes for the beautiful: in any case it is very imperfectly successful. What I care for is the beautiful itself and the vision of the beautiful, in so far as they manage to exist, or to be suggested: and this frail, intermittent, but actual realization of the beautiful I call the spiritual sphere. All life is, intrinsically, a part of it; but horribly interrupted and perturbed.

'Yours sincerely,
'G. SANTAYANA.'

26

AE was a most voluminous letter-writer, especially after he had given up the *Irish Statesman*. 'I managed', he tells St. John Ervine, 'to store up enough energy in the first seven years of my life, which I spent in Ulster, to enable me to answer letters ever afterwards.' His letters, of which there

A Memoir of AE

must be many hundreds besides those which kind friends have sent for the purposes of this Memoir, are of so even a quality that selection is difficult: he is perhaps at his best in those he wrote to his American friend Kingsley Porter, a distinguished archaeologist, collected by Mrs. Porter in one of the most pleasing little volumes of which AE has been the author or occasion.[1] This friendship it probably was which detained AE in Ireland after his wife's death, and he made repeated visits to the Porters, first at Marble Hill which they had rented from the Laws, and afterwards at Glenveagh Castle, a lonely mansion situated fifteen miles inland from the coast opposite Tory Island, which had lain derelict for twenty years until Kingsley Porter took a fancy to it. AE was strongly attracted to Kingsley Porter, who conceived for AE one of those devoted attachments which the latter was always capable of inspiring. On the day before his death he wrote a letter to AE, ending with the words: 'You and Donegal are, we feel, the best the world has to offer'. We infer his character from the passages in which AE rallies him on his pessimism, his hatred of mechanism, his delight in rainy days, and even pokes mild fun at

[1] *AE's Letters to Mínanlábáin*, with an Introduction by Lucy Kingsley Porter (New York, Macmillan, 1937).

the Christian antiquities which are the subject of his friend's investigations. 'When I think of all the harm that old clergyman Patrick did by his blundering zeal I can never forgive him.' In another letter, on the theme ' our own age fits us like a glove ', AE shows that he himself is not wholly indifferent to the comforts of civilisation :

' Please Heaven, none of these solutions [Communism, etc.] will come in my time, as I hope the system will last out my life. I grew up under it and am accustomed to it. And I could not stand the highly organised machine state whether capitalist or communist, and I would feel horribly uncomfortable in a Mexican world of primitive cobblers and weavers. I can't imagine any country or place quite so fitted for my failings as my own country and my own location. I don't think I would have liked the sanitary arrangements of ancient Athens, though I should have delighted in the society of Plato and Aristophanes and Socrates. I believe the smells in Chinese cities are worse, and that disposes of a yearning to have lived close to Laotze. I have read accounts of Hindu yogis and I cannot with my temperament see myself with a beggar's bowl following after Buddha. Yes, I am where I ought to be, the

A Memoir of AE

imperfect peg in the imperfect hole which it fits perfectly.'

With his new friends AE could always be sure of what he most required, an audience; for there was usually a crowd of visitors, and Kingsley Porter never seemed to have too much of his talk. Mrs. Porter has an amusing picture of an evening at Marble Hill :

' AE did not come to dine with us again. He found it stuffy indoors and a tedious waste of time. So he came instead to afternoon tea, staying on to talk with us on the terrace. Our guests were too much engrossed to notice the passing of time. When dinner was announced we invited him in. He would not come, neither would he stop talking. As there was no end to a paragraph I could not break in. The soup got cold on the table. The household became restive. They made violent signs behind his back for me to stop him. But AE, all unconscious, talked on. At this point Kingsley saved the situation and the dinner by sauntering off with AE who still under full steam continued his conversation.'

We have another glimpse of him, at Glenveagh Castle, in a letter from one of his fellow-guests, Walter Muir Whitehill :

A Memoir of AE

'The evenings were given over to sonorous monologues by AE on every possible subject. On fine days he would go out to paint, and I generally went with him, for he could talk, paint and smoke his pipe simultaneously. On rainy days he installed himself in an unfurnished room where fishing-tackle was kept, and worked over the paintings begun on fine days. He brought a few soap-boxes into this room for use as chairs, and claimed to prefer it because matches could be thrown on the floor freely. Here there was more talk and friendly quarrelling, in which he playfully tried to convert me from mediaeval archaeology to painting. When he left on 19th August, 1932, he, to our great delight, gave us one of the best paintings he had done during his visit—a bit of the shore just below Glenveagh Castle.'

Kingsley Porter loved the sea, and had built a cottage on Inishbofin, the nearest island of the Tory archipelago to the coast. On 7th July, 1933, he had written to AE, saying that he and Mrs. Porter were going to spend the night on the island and would return on the following day, when AE was expected to meet them on the mainland. In the morning Porter went out on the cliffs of Inishbofin, and was never seen again. A violent thunderstorm raged all day. Mrs. Porter tells how as her boat approached the mainland that evening she saw ' a tall figure standing on the rocks beside our faithful chauffeur '. Russell was calm and helpful, thinking of everything that should be done, and as the Sergeant of the Civic Guards was away he ' practically conducted the preliminary inquest '. ' But no physical sign of Kingsley was ever again to be found.'

AE remained for a while at Glenveagh, and Mrs. Porter has a touching account of his watchful sympathy. It was the trouble of others which best revealed in him those qualities which endeared him to his friends. He had brought with him an advance copy of *The Avatars*, and ' sitting on the very edge of a large comfortable upholstered armchair, so that I felt he would surely slip off, he would read until he had to stop to light the lamp. Then he would continue, peering at me from time to time over the top of his spectacles, tenderly as a mother, hoping I had fallen asleep.'

27

Just before leaving for Glenveagh he had written to Weekes to find him rooms in London :

A Memoir of AE

'My house is at present being emptied and all in it sold. I am keeping only a few pictures and a few books. I don't want to gather possessions. I want to be mobile and not tied to things. I had begun to feel I was in a rut. I want to break up the mould of mind in which I was decaying. I think the change will reinvigorate me, and it will be a relief to get away from Ireland in its present mood, which is one of smugness.'

And he quoted from one of his favourite poems, Tennyson's ' Ulysses ' :

> Old age hath yet his honour and his toil.

Seumas O'Sullivan—to whom I have been indebted for materials in writing this Memoir—took over from him an accumulation of books, letters and MSS. ; and Mrs. Coates (Carrie Rea)—to whom also I am indebted—who was with him when he was clearing out his house, tells me that he gave much of the furniture and £100 to the servant who had been his faithful attendant. Weekes found him rooms at 41 Sussex Gardens, Hyde Park, where he stayed till April of the following year (1934). Of his general plans he writes soon after his arrival to Arnold Marsh of Waterford :

'It was kind of you to write as you did. But Ireland does not lose anything by my departure.

A Memoir of AE

I have given everything to it I had to give and there is nothing left, no idea of any value. I do not say I have gone altogether. After my wife's death I had a house on my hands which I did not want, and I also felt I was getting into a rut, so before I became feeble in will I uprooted myself, got rid of all my impedimenta except shirts, collars, etc., and a few books, and became mobile so that I could move anywhere with little trouble. I came here first because I had a number of old friends I wanted to meet again and compare wisdoms since we parted. After a while I may go to U.S.A., where I have a son married to a very nice girl, and they want me to migrate. I think they feel I am getting elderly and will soon not be able to look after myself. I am not that old yet however. I may in a year return to Dublin and live in lodgings so that I can if I want go to Donegal for three or four months in the summer. I could not afford to do that and keep a house as well. It is all very vague. But I will be here for some months, and so soon as the weather gets cooler I will try to start on a new book. I would be glad to believe that anything I have written may be read hereafter by a generation of Irish more concerned about the deeps than the surface of life. I sometimes believe this, and

A Memoir of AE

that I had things to say which would not be passed by. But this may not be a critical unbiassed judgment, but only vanity lurking somewhere inside me. Anyhow, the present generation does not care a rap about my mysticism, and it is quite possible the generation after that may care no more, but be bored, as our people like surface activities and brilliances and the silences do not allure them. I have no wounded feelings of any kind. I never desired personal glory of any kind, and the only real pleasures I desired were the understanding of some four or five people who were on the same path as myself. You will see how remote I am in mind from the present generation if you read a book of mine *The Avatars*, which Macmillan will publish in October.'

It was a great belief with AE that there is a 'law of spiritual gravitation' which, at the proper moment, brings people together. 'I sought out nobody when I came here', he tells Van Wyck Brooks, 'but allowed the law to operate, and in a few weeks I had plenty of intimates.' His regular haunt was the National Gallery, and he would make appointments at its doors. Some of those of whom we hear most in his letters are the Baxes, Orage,

A Memoir of AE

Herbert Palmer, Ruth Pitter ('whom I think the best of living English poetesses'), Sir William Rothenstein, A. L. Rowse, Mrs. Constance Sitwell, Pamela Travers, Helen Waddell. James Stephens, on whose company he had reckoned, was absent in America. The career of Orage had run curiously parallel to his own, first as an ardent Theosophist, then as editor of a brilliant weekly journal; until, about middle age, feeling the need of reaffirming to himself his spiritual faith, he had subjected himself to the discipline of Gurdjieff at Fontainebleau and in the United States; from this influence he had emerged with a weakened faith in the capacity of the human intelligence for transcendental certitude, and had thrown all his energies into advocacy of the Douglas Credit scheme, which he now persuaded himself and others that Roosevelt was about to adopt in America. 'Is there anything in it?' AE enquires of Ernest Boyd. 'You know Orage's way of hinting. I will sound him about it. Orage is too sure about everything. He hypnotises many of his readers by an air of intellectual surety. But is humanity to be saved so easily!' Philip Mairet writes:

'They met regularly every week about 4 in the afternoon, generally at the Kardomah

A Memoir of AE

Café in Chancery Lane, and there was evidently a very close understanding between them: mainly upon such topics as Indian philosophy, Yogi practices and higher religious thought generally, with frequent excursions into literature, Irish and general. Orage used to speak of these conversations, and I was present at one of them, but often they were alone together. . . . Orage died suddenly on the night of Nov. 5-6, and on the 6th I had to break the news to AE, who called at the office to see Orage by appointment. I believe it was a serious blow to him, for these weekly meetings had become a spiritual resource to both of these distinguished men. He wrote [for the *New English Weekly*] a very beautiful memorial article on " the mind of Orage ".'

The cold reception of *The Avatars* was a disappointment to him, though he was cheered by appreciative letters from Helen Waddell, Sir W. Rothenstein and others. A letter of October to Seán O'Faoláin may be quoted, as it alludes to this subject; also it is a commentary on that line of his verse into which as he said he had put most meaning:

All our thoughts are throngs of living souls.

A Memoir of AE

'I think with many others that the universe we see is made by the congregation of spirits which inhabit it as they again live and have their being in an incomprehensible Absolute. We have imagined ourselves into littleness, darkness, and ignorance, and we have to imagine ourselves back into light. I may misapply my own philosophy, and there may be, probably are, a million better ways of applying it than any I know. But I have written nothing except out of some mood which had made the psyche momentarily luminous. I have not power enough to make a great fire, and I emit a thin light, but that effort at transfiguration of the opacity into luminousness is what the Indians would call my Dharma. They think for everyone there is a special work and even if it does not appear to be great it is best for that person, and they say " the Dharma of another is full of danger ". That is, if I, seeing how great the work of another is, desert my own work to labour as that other does, I am losing my way in life. I never blame those whose way is different. I believe in freedom, and if I blame any I deny them essential freedom and I wrong them. I can see a thousand ways to light in the paths others travel. It is quite possible that those

A Memoir of AE

who contemplate with sympathy myriads of diverse characters, as novelists like Dostoevsky or Tolstoi or Balzac or poets like Shakspeare, are more than any travelling on the straight path. As the perfection of the body is to mirror an external nature in itself, so I think the perfection of the psyche is to mirror all life in itself, so that our thoughts will become throngs of living souls. And if you choose to depict with sympathy and understanding the lives of the people you know you may be far ahead of me in my effort to create or emit a light which I think spiritual.

' *The Avatars* is the book of an oldish man whose light is flickering, and whose mind has become a little blurred. I read it after it came out and see how uncertain it is in its art. But it may give some illumination to those who read my other books. Anyhow there are so many books with a great light in them that if mine fails to give any light it does not matter. The world will be no darker, and I really do not care very much about praise or recognition. I am rejoicing at present in being a wanderer, the cries of my race no longer touching me, the lights of love and home long behind me, and drowned in hazes of sunken years. I like the sensation of freedom, that none puts a delaying hand on me, and I can, like the Indians, after being a householder retire to the jungle to meditate.'

He was in Dublin again at Christmas, staying with his old friend Seumas O'Sullivan ; he even seems to have had some thoughts of settling there again. At other times he thought of travelling round the world. But AE, though he surprised one occasionally by the things he noticed, was not in general interested enough in external things to make a good travelling psychologist of the type of Keyserling ; and the 'spiritual gravitation' of London still prevailed. Most of his friends were there now, and in London he was almost as near Heaven (*i.e.* Donegal) as in Dublin. Several of the younger poets there looked to him for counsel and direction. Here, for instance, is advice to Herbert Palmer, a poet whose verse he admired, though he was doubtful of the principle on which much of Palmer's verse is written, ' facit indignatio versum'.

' I am a gentle creature and look with terror on the wrath of God, which is the attitude of deity you feel inspired by. I have no doubt that there is a divine wrath. Many poets have been inspired

A Memoir of AE

by it: Dante, Shelley in his political poetry, Dryden and Pope, though I am sometimes dubious about the last two, whether the Devil has not as much to do with the wrath as God. When I was young I loved Laotze, who said, " To be gentle is to be invincible ", and though I allowed myself to be inspired by the wrath at odd times and had a sneaking admiration for the result, I generally felt ashamed after these outbursts. But I can enjoy others committing the sin of righteous rage, and I hope your verse will make the monster turn up its white belly, and that you will then come to gentleness in yourself once more.'

In another letter to the same poet occurs the striking sentence:

' There are two points in our lives never to be spoken of: the highest, which is sacred, and to speak of it would turn earthwards the soaring meditative spirit; and there is the depth in us which we never speak of for pity's sake; " it must never, never be sung ".'

In March 1934 he decided to spend the summer in Donegal. I quote part of a long letter to Van Wyck Brooks, in which he gives some account of this, his last visit there:

A Memoir of AE

c/o Mrs. Margaret O'Donnell,
Parkmore, (?)
Ballymore,
Co. Donegal
29/5/34

'How delightful of you to send me your Essays on America. They followed me here where I have taken a cottage for three months, May, June and July. I was in London for nine months—though I had many good friends there I fled from it. I could not endure asphalt underfoot and fog and mist overhead. I wanted real unspoiled nature and came to this adorable country, partly to write a poem a little long for me, partly to paint, which is my recreation, and mainly to idle, which I am entitled to do as I am close on seventy. But when one has used one's mind it gets the habit of working, and doubtless you will discover when you are old and think of idling that your mind won't let you. My painting alas is not satisfactory as my sight is not as good as it used to be. I can still imagine, but alas I cannot draw precisely, as doubtless you saw in the little sketch on the other side. Your work was a godsend. I brought nothing with me except a twelve-volume translation of the *Mahabharata* which I got from India. It is marvellous, a whole literature in itself, cosmic myths, two sacred books, endless stories, treatises on government, magic philosophy and the great epic itself. But though I love the book it becomes at times—how shall I describe it—in Thoreau's phrase, when he was asked why he left Walden, "Perhaps there was a little languor in the afternoons". Well, reading about two or three thousand years ago tends in our weaker moments to a little languor in the afternoons and one longs for contemporary thought, and your delightful essays came to relieve the weakness of my spirit and I fell on them with enthusiasm. I think they are the best thinking you have done that I know about. After my visits to U.S.A. I could understand better. I noted delightful things page after page. How good that sentence about Heine is, that he possessed the secret of being impudent for eternity. I marked sentence after sentence. " Everything that springs from solitude shines by a light of its own ", and your description of American university graduates " consistently educated in twin values that are incompatible ". And I gave an appreciative chuckle over the wisdom " Tammany has as much to teach Good Government as Good Government has to teach Tammany ". I could go on for pages sending

A Memoir of AE

back your wisdom to yourself but that would be the cheapest return for your gift. I feel one thing specially to be good, true and wise. You suggest to the artist and poet voluntary poverty. We are all poor in Ireland and it has done none of us any harm. The happiest years of my life were when I was young and lived on less than fifty pounds a year, and could afford no luxuries. But we sat up to all hours talking about everything in heaven and earth, and we brooded and brooded on what we read. I live now very economically, as my fixed income is about £100 a year, and am I unhappy? Good God, no. I feel like Swedenborg's angels who were continually advancing to the springtime of their youth, that is, inside I feel like that. Outside, alas, I cannot climb hills the way I used to. But I feel sure you are right. So many artists want a motor-car, a house, to give parties, etc., that they sell their genius for cash. They should all take the vow of poverty that is an inside vow. It does not mean that if somebody leaves them 100,000 dollars in a will, they refuse it, but that they stand ready at any time to desert prosperity if it conflicts with the spirit. I started doing this when my father found me a well-paid job. I gave it up as my ethical sense was outraged and then for about

A Memoir of AE

six years I lived with an income varying from thirty to sixty pounds and was magnificently happy. Yeats had long years of poverty and never sold his talent. Stephens was living on one pound a week when he wrote *The Charwoman's Daughter* and *The Crock of Gold* and the early poems. Stephen MacKenna, the translator of Plotinus, the greatest piece of prose written in our time I think, lived at the end of his life in a cottage on two pounds a week and refused a good income rather than undertake work he did not like. All my Irish literary friends are poor except Lord Dunsany, who was born with an income, and Yeats, who in his old age became famous, so that people had to buy his books as a duty. It is quite easy to be poor. The needs of life, I think Emerson says, are much fewer than most people suppose. The two great needs are good talk and plenty of solitude to brood and dig deep, and both can be had here at least. Even in this out of the way place, with no town and only cottages, I find good talk. This morning on the shore from ten to one I talked with a man who like myself found out this place and took a room, and we discussed Eastern philosophy, the architecture of dream, the anima mundi and other things and parted with regret. Yes, preach poverty to the artists. Voluntary poverty is better than poverty thrust upon them, as it is at present I fancy in your country. But I think the American soul is waking. It will be roused by sorrow, and when one deep is sounded all the other deeps call.'

The poem mentioned in this letter is "The House of the Titans", one of his most ambitious attempts, though not one of his successes. It lacks a clear outline—a fatal defect in a poem aiming at the epic manner—and he seems to have wearied of it, as Keats wearied of *Hyperion*, of which it is reminiscent. A poem more generally interesting, though when published with the first at the end of the year, it attracted less attention than perhaps it deserved, was 'The Dark Lady'. He was proud of this poem, for in it he claimed to have made an important contribution to the solution of the riddle of Shakspeare's Sonnets. It was the result of a meditation on the sands one day in Donegal, probably on his favourite theme of the nature of the creative activity of the poet and artist. 'I wrote this poem to illustrate my belief that Shakspeare was so sensitive that by affinities the souls of the living and the dead breathed their life into him ; he may have thought they were imagina-

A Memoir of AE

tions, and dressed them up as kings or villains.' The quotation is from a letter to H. F. Norman, in which he told how the conception of the poem came to him :

' " The Dark Lady " is a queer thing. I never believed the Dark Lady was the sensual creature most interpreters assumed. I did not know the Sonnets very well, but last spring I started a meditation about Shakspeare and the Dark Lady, and I woke up in the middle of sleep with a high lucid moment. The Dark Lady was breathing into my soul a most poignant tale, breathing her very being into mine. As usual, the next morning I could remember nothing but the memory of having heard or felt some marvellous story. Then in Donegal last June it all came into my mind as I was meditating on the sands, and I wrote it off with the greatest ease, and then before including it in the book, I thought I would read the Sonnets, which I hardly knew, and found what I think is confirmation.'

He quotes several curious passages in the Sonnets ; but I must say that if AE was really chosen to be the Oedipus of the great riddle, he hardly deserved the glory, for he had often shocked me by avowing his detestation of the Sonnets !

A Memoir of AE

Other authors besides Shakspeare suggested to AE similar speculations. His friend Joseph O'Neill, a high official in the Education Department of the Irish Free State, had astonished all his friends by producing *Wind from the North,* a novel of Danish times in Dublin, which revealed a singular power of entering into the past.

'I think your story of the Norse is not an ancestral memory, but a personal memory of some kind breaking through. I always thought that theory of ancestral memories unscientific. Some remote ancestor of yours lived in Dublin at the time of Brian; rays or waves of light reflected from the city and its people converged on the optic nerve; the vibrations ran to the brain cells, then when he married the vibrations ran down into the germ cell and grew up in his child, and so were passed on until they emerged again in full consciousness in Joseph O'Neill. I think the doctrine ludicrous. An unchanging image cannot be maintained in an ever-changing substance, and the original images must have been jolted to pieces in the nine hundred years since Joseph O'Neill's ancestor was in love with Gudrun and went baresark. Give the preposterous theory up and believe with three quarters of the human race that you have lived before and will always live. If you want the finest logic and reason brought to bear on the problem read MacTaggart, the greatest of English philosophers, upon "The Doctrine of Pre-Existence". Yeats thinks he is the only English philosopher worth the name. You will be in good company with the great Avatars, Buddha, Krishna, with philosophers like Plato and Plotinus, with poets like Goethe, Hugo, Wordsworth, Tennyson, Vaughan, Emerson, Whitman, Shelley, and a score of others, and in believing this you will have grown up in mind and will get an age in your thought. This is the "Ancestral Wisdom" which Keats said was in every man. You tap your past memories, my friend, what wells up within you as imaginations, and you will get stories innumerable.'

And he reverts to Shakspeare's Sonnets :

'My idea is that Shakspeare was in half-conscious contact with other souls. . . . I had the idea in my first poems in *Homeward Songs*, when I wrote :

All my thoughts are throngs of living souls.

I have " frequent been with unknown minds ", but never tried to tell in my own words what that interpretation meant until I had the imagination of "The Dark Lady". All kinds of profundities, illuminations and intuitions meet us in the depths of meditation.'

In Donegal there was a brief revival of his practical interest in the 'National Being'. He was asked for his advice about the constitution of the Senate, and in a letter to Mrs. Erskine Childers he advocated a non-political Second Chamber—a 'fountain of expert opinion' on technical matters—which should stand for the 'bodily life' of the country as the national parliament stood for its 'soul'. This letter was duly considered by President De Valera, but I am unable to say whether it was found of practical service.

He was back in London at the end of July 1934, in rooms at 1 Brunswick Square. Ireland, he tells Pamela Travers, had been rather sad for him, so many of his friends had died or left it.

'But I love the country itself and feel unhappy outside it. Here I have a good many friends to whom I can talk about anything, but the country itself is dead to me, and no breath from the Kalini blows in its winds or from the occult nature. I feel like somebody adrift in a boat which carries him half imperceptibly away from the familiar shore to some empty space in the waters.'

But he was to have one experience of the beauty of English landscape at the house of his friend Mrs. Constance Sitwell, in Northumberland, whom he visited in September 1934. Mrs. Sitwell kindly contributes some notes on this visit :

' After the first day or so, when he felt the air light and invigorating, and had shaken off the heaviness, as he called it, of London and the South of England, a deep gaiety seemed to take possession of him. In the mornings he sat in a glade of trees by himself with his pipe, filling page after page of his sketch-book with lovely figures. . . . One day we went to look at Norham. The place looked beautiful, with the Tweed flowing glittering below ; the sun was hot and the Castle stood up, all a warm pink, in the bright grass. He sat on a bank and did a sketch of it with extraordinary rapidity. . . . Another day we went to see a little waterfall. He looked around with joy at the wide and empty moor on the way there, saying it was like part of Donegal. We found some stones with ancient markings, circular and cup-marked, which interested him, but he said it would take some time before he would be able to "see" anything. He had his sketch-book with him, but instead of drawing the waterfall he said he would draw me : he wasn't pleased with his work, saying his eyes were not good enough for fine drawing now (which wasn't true).... On the last day of his visit we went to the shore ; walking through the sand-dunes one comes suddenly on the beach ; there was a bank of violet cloud, deep in colour, lying over the sea with a line of the clearest lemon light along the horizon above the green water. He seemed possessed by joy, and said it was the most beautiful colour he had seen out of Ireland.

'One evening it was about the intuitions he had had of his own incarnations that he talked. "They tell me that my recollections and visions are ancestral memories—a mere phrase. I talked to Julian Huxley about it once. You tell me, I said, that a man cannot transmit musical knowledge, or a language he has mastered, or a craft, to his children ? No, he said, you may transmit a tendency, but everything has to be learnt afresh. And yet you tell me, I said, that when I get a glimpse of strange cities and buildings I have never seen, vivid and alive in every detail, the figures in the streets, the sharp shadows, it has nothing to do with me, but is a memory of some hypothetical ancestor of mine who may have gone on the Crusades? Huxley didn't know what to say. He told me he had sat up all night once trying to find a flaw in one of my arguments, and had to give it up!"

'He often talked of death, saying that if he was told he had an incurable disease he would be very excited at the thought of going on as to a new great adventure and would prepare for the journey with a thrill—that he wasn't in the least frightened of death—all that he objected to was being what he called " thrust out of the body " instead of leaving it when one chose.'

Such an announcement was presently to be made to him.

28

But for AE as for Ulysses in his favourite poem,

'Twas not too late to seek a newer world.

In November he received a cable from the U.S. Department of Agriculture requesting him to 'come and advise about some rural policies'. He was not feeling very well, but he 'capitulated after the sixth cable', and in December he set off

A Memoir of AE

to New York from Southampton. A letter to Joseph O'Neill is dated 'R.M.S. *Aurania*, Christmas':

'Here I am at Halifax when I should have been in New York two days ago. But the weather was terrific and the seas running to mountains, and we had to go slow lest the back of the ship be broken on the bumping waves, and we had to go a hundred miles out of our course on a wireless call to help rescue a sinking ship. It was the strangest sight. Four great liners came up at midnight and stood round the battered Swedish vessel sinking. Searchlights playing over a waste of moonlight waters and wild foam. No boat could go out to the sinking ship until this *Aurania* let loose a flood of oil which was blown over the surface to the sinking vessel and then the boats from another liner could put off. A little after the rescue the ship sank. I seem fated to meet adventures. Luckily I am immune against sea-sickness and enjoy the wild waters. Met some interesting folk on board, one in especial who has been photographing Canada from the air up to the Arctic Circle, making maps out of them and very many discoveries while doing it. They can now tell from the air where minerals, radium, gold, iron, etc., are likely to be found. They use infra-red rays, and find all the cracks in the earth where the interior molten stuff boiled through and left mineral deposits, and they can find the movement of glaciers in the Ice Age. It is a strange business this reading of the earth and its past history from the air. They have already taken over seven hundred thousand photographs. Lord, what a waste of wild earth near the Arctic Circle. Places never visited by humanity before. Very dangerous work, too. My expert, who had charge of this mapping from the air, crashed some months ago and escaped miraculously with only a broken knee-cap and a deaf ear and the loss of his front teeth, while two others were killed. But he is eager for more discoveries. He was returning from lecturing in Paris and London on this new art of reading the world from the sky and the revelations made possible now about the skin of the earth. I expect to get to New York Thursday, but I hope not to be long over on this side.'

On landing he went straight to Washington and was at once at the heart of things in the States and of all the excitement of relief schemes for the

20,000,000 unemployed. He had talks with the President, whom he 'liked', and who interested AE particularly by his account of how 'stranded artists were set to decorate schools and public buildings', receiving a subsistence allowance and the paints and canvases. 'I wish I was a stranded American artist to take part in this.' He conferred with the Minister of Labour, with Collier—the Commissioner for Indian Affairs—and with many others. But the man who most attracted him was Henry Wallace, Secretary of the Department of Agriculture, 'the best brain in the Administration and an old friend of mine. He has loomed up since I was here before as the dominating figure in the Roosevelt administration.' Mr. Wallace, it may be remembered, as a young man had called on AE at the office of the *Irish Homestead*, and he had been much impressed, as he told in a speech delivered after AE's death, by

'a prophetic statement written in 1915 in which AE declared the inevitability of the greater role of the State in the life of the individual. AE was not a statistician, nor a classical economist, but in his preoccupation with the intangibles which give beauty and direction to life, he nevertheless had a sense of social trends.'

A Memoir of AE

To Wallace AE wrote during this tour:

'I see some of that universalism or planetary consciousness in you which I think I told you was to be the root-idea in the Spenglerian sense in this country, and your wish for a religious mood which would embrace Buddhists, Christians and the rest is an expression of that planetary consciousness coming out in thought; and again when you say that the origin and destiny of this country have more in common with this ultimate Catholicity of world-religious purpose than most have been willing to admit, you are impelled by the root-idea of the American culture. And it is clear again when you feel the destiny of the world is towards a far greater unity than we now enjoy. It is I think impossible for you as a public man to go further than that at the moment, as you have such heavy material obligations laid on you. But I am sure there will come a time when you will speak more fully out of that evolving world-consciousness, and set the minds of your people to brood upon its destiny. The destiny of no creature or state can be for itself only. I hope to see you when I get back to Washington and we may talk over this and other ideas.'

A Memoir of AE

He stayed in Washington at the Cosmos Club, 'mainly composed of artists, writers and scientists', and a room was given him at the Department of Agriculture, where each day he interviewed 'groups of experts'. 'Here I am', he writes to Weekes, 'quite different from the AE you knew forty years ago, a bold creature, facing administrators and economists, and finding that they are impressed : I wish I could be as impressed by myself.' What was novel in him as an economist, he was told, was that he never forgot that man was a human being. They all seemed to know his *National Being*. Sometimes, after one of his discourses, they would ask him to recite his poetry to them, and nothing loth he would intone it forth. He would have enjoyed it all to the full but for his health : he had begun to complain of being ' tired out '.

A pleasing interlude in this American mission was a visit to his son in Chicago. ' I found him well, with an enchanting American girl, his wife, who looks like a fairy princess, and is as kind, good and natural as she could be. She is rather a lover of my poetry, and Diarmuid says she married him because he was my son, but I think he is good enough to be liked and accepted for his own sake.'

A Memoir of AE

The second and more interesting part of his mission remained. He writes to Weekes, 29th January, 1935:

'I have been asked to go to New Mexico and Arizona to meet the Indian nations on reservations, and explain co-operative ideals to them. The U.S.A. is making these Indians self-governing on their reservations and many of them maintain ancient languages and religions of a rather profound pantheistic character—nature, its works, trees, earth, lakes, clouds are Being to them, and the head of the Indian Department, a mystic himself, thought I, as a mystic, could explain better to them the application of co-operative methods to their arts and crafts than a mere official economist. I have not decided to go as it is rather an exhausting labour for a man of my age. But it would be fascinating to meet these survivals of the old nature cults. You can see I am having an exciting time in this most exciting of capitals. Everybody is, in a sense, exhilarated by the national emergency and rises to it, while a few gloomy Republicans foresee disaster.'

He was strongly tempted by the 'romance' of this adventure, and was deciding to yield to the temptation, when he suddenly became really ill. Dreading to be laid up in a strange city, he hurriedly left Washington, and set off homeward at the beginning of March.

29

He suffered much during the return journey. In London, where he changed his lodgings to 14 Tavistock Place, his doctor diagnosed his ailment as colitis, and ' put him on a pallid diet of soda and milk, barley-water, junket and such-like things '. A bacteriological examination was deemed satisfactory.

In a letter to Henry Wallace he describes his condition (23rd April):

> 'I am here under doctor's control. They found I had some inflammation in my colon or other internal apparatus, and I have been put on the most pallid diet, and have been washed out inside. But the drastic treatment is making me better already. But I am as limp in mind and body as I could be. It was that which made me so uninspired and fireless at Washington. But it was as well I came away, for I would have been laid up in that strange city where I only

know you and Lewis Chase. Here my friends pour in upon me in the afternoons or evenings to condole. . . . I am doing nothing except trying to keep warm as my diet has no heat powers in it. I read books which do not interest me. I have read too many in my life, and Eddington's last book appears fantastically unreal as indeed most scientific books appear. When I am well enough I will go to Donegal and begin again my old worship of nature. Here it is difficult to worship it under asphalt pavements.'

He still talked with something of his old fire to his visitors, and wrote many letters. Preparations for the Jubilee celebrations were in progress, and in his comment to an Irish friend, AE's old feeling of antipathy to things English appears to have been slightly modified :

' London is getting decorative. What is Yeats's phrase about " new commonness upon the throne, the crowd hanging its paper flowers from post to post " ? But royalty does mean something over here. A solid thing in which they put their trust, and on the whole this people have come better out of their troubles than any other by sticking to their traditions and conventions.'

A Memoir of AE

And again :

'I wish we could change De Valera, the abstractionist, for Stanley Baldwin, the human being. Lord, how we want a natural kind human being at the head of Irish affairs.'

His chief interest was in preparing his *Selected Poems* for Macmillan ; and in this task he turned to the friend of his youth, Charles Weekes, who was thus associated with AE's last volume of poems as he had been with the first.

As his health did not improve, Weekes grew anxious about him : there was a further medical examination, and a change from London was recommended. In the middle of June I was surprised to receive from him a letter announcing that he was coming to Bournemouth, where a suitable place had been found for him. I had not seen him for many years (I had fancied that he had never been quite the same to me since our wretched tiff on the tramcar in Dublin !), and when Weekes brought him down on 21st June, I found less change in him than others who had known him during the intervening period : he was thin again, and more like the Russell of earlier years. The weather was beautiful, and he lay all day in a deck-chair under the trees. Sometimes I would find him half-asleep,

A Memoir of AE

but he was always ready to start up and talk, much in his old style. He did not yet know how ill he was, and talked to my wife of his confidence that three months in Donegal would cure him. Then one day when I called I was told he was not so well and was in bed; he seemed intermittently in pain and was too tired to talk, except to tell me, with almost excited pleasure, of the medal which the Irish Academy of Letters had just awarded him. It was on this occasion that he asked me to bring him a copy of Tennyson. Next day, a doctor had been called in to see him, and had advised a consultation. 'He says he doesn't think it's cancer', said AE, 'but I really don't care.' His London friends were now informed of his condition, and Pamela Travers was a great comfort to him when she arrived, writing his letters for him and attending him constantly. He was moved to a Nursing Home for an operation, and when I saw him after it his face was quite changed, and it was plain that the end was near. Friends had assembled, Helen Waddell, Weekes, Constantine Curran, and others, and just at the end Oliver Gogarty arrived from Dublin. One by one we went up to him to say what was really good-bye. His son Diarmuid had been sent for, but it was too late. He was pathetically anxious to hear from Yeats, to whom several messages were sent, and happily a letter arrived in time for it to be read to him. Certainly no one could face death in a spirit more becoming to a man. On the night of 17th July, after Gogarty's visit, writes Pamela Travers, ' he asked for a drink and was even able to move his pillow into a more comfortable position. About eleven o'clock he fell into a deep, calm, even sleep, and soon after that he died.'

Of the many tributes called forth by the announcement of AE's death, Lord Dunsany's lines best convey the impression of unworldly goodness he left on all who knew him :

> A lovely radiance of a passing star
>   Upon a sudden journey through the gloaming,
> Lighting low Irish hills, and then afar
>   To its own regions homing.

In Dublin, on Saturday 20th July, there was a great gathering round his grave in Mount Jerome Cemetery : the most prominent figures perhaps were President De Valera and the High Poet of Erin, W. B. Yeats. Frank O'Connor read an impressive oration. But the most eloquent testimony of grief and admiration was one not reported in the newspapers. Amongst those present was a woman who had been in service with the Russells soon after their marriage, and presently it became evident that she had 'got into trouble'. She was not dismissed, however, and was looked after. She now placed on the grave a large mass of flowers, 'very precious', and when someone spoke to her of what they must have cost she answered : ' I would have died for him '.

I

AE'S WRITINGS

To the Fellows of the Theosophical Society. *Leaflet of 8 pp.* 'The Irish Theosophist' Press, 1894.
Homeward : Songs by the Way. Dublin, Whaley, 1894.
The Future of Ireland and the Awakening of the Fires. *Pamphlet.* Dublin, 1897.
Ideals in Ireland : Priest or Hero ? *Pamphlet.* Dublin, 1897.
The Earth Breath and other poems. New York and London, John Lane, 1897.
Literary Ideals in Ireland [*in collaboration*]. Dublin, 'Daily Express', 1899.
Ideals in Ireland [*in collaboration*]. Dublin, 1901.
The Divine Vision, and other poems. Macmillan, 1903.
The Nuts of Knowledge, lyrical poems. Dun Emer Press, 1903.
Controversy in Ireland : an appeal to Irish journalists. *12 pp.* Dublin, O'Donoghue, 1904.
The Mask of Apollo, and other stories. Dublin, 1904.
Some Irish Essays. (Tower Press Booklets.) Dublin, 1906.
By Still Waters, lyrical poems old and new. Dun Emer Press, 1906.
Deirdre, a drama in three acts. (Tower Press Booklets, Second Series.) Dublin, 1907.
The Hero in Man. London, The Orpheus Press, 1909.
The Building up of a Rural Civilisation : an address. *12 pp.* Dublin, 1910.

A Memoir of AE

The Renewal of Youth. London, The Orpheus Press, 1911.

Co-operation and Nationality. Dublin, Maunsel, 1912.

The Dublin Strike. A speech delivered in the Royal Albert Hall. *8 pp.* London, Christian Commonwealth Company, 1913.

The Tragedy of Labour in Dublin. *Single sheet.* Reprint from 'The Times', Nov. 13, 1913.

To the Masters of Dublin. *Sm. 4to broadside.* Reprint from 'The Irish Times', Oct. 7, 1913.

Collected Poems. Macmillan, 1913.

The Rural Community: an address. Dublin, The Plunkett House, 1913.

Gods of War, and other poems. Dublin, 1915.

Imaginations and Reveries. Dublin and London, Maunsel, 1915.

Templecrone: a record of Co-operative effort. *Leaflet.* Dublin, reprint from 'The Irish Homestead', 1916.

Ireland, Agriculture and the War. An open letter to Irish farmers. *Pamphlet.* Dublin, 1916.

Talks with an Irish Farmer. *8 pp.* Reprint from 'The Irish Homestead', 1916.

The National Being. Dublin and London, Maunsel, 1916.

Salutation, a poem on the Irish Rebellion of 1916. *12 pp.* London, 25 copies printed by Clement Shorter, 1917.

Thoughts for a Convention. Dublin and London, Maunsel, 1917.

Conscription for Ireland: a warning to England. *4 pp.* Dublin, 1918.

The Candle of Vision. London, Macmillan, 1918.

A Plea for Justice, being a demand for a public enquiry into the attacks on the Co-operative Societies in Ireland. Dublin, 'The Irish Homestead', 1920.

A Memoir of AE

The Economics of Ireland. (The Freeman Pamphlets.) New York, 1921.
The Inner and the Outer Ireland. Reprint from 'Pearson's Magazine'. Dublin, Talbot Press, 1921.
Ireland and the Empire at the Court of Conscience. Dublin, Talbot Press, 1921.
Ireland, Past and Future. A paper read to the Sociological Society, Feb. 1922.
The Interpreters. London, Macmillan, 1922.
Voices of the Stones [Poems]. London, Macmillan, 1925.
Midsummer Eve [Poem.] New York, Crosbie Gaige, 1928.
Dark Weeping. (The Ariel Poems.) London, Faber and Faber, 1929.
Enchantment, and other poems. New York, Fountain Press, 1930.
Vale, and other poems. New York, Macmillan, 1931.
Verses for Friends. Dublin, 25 copies printed for the writer, 1932.
Song and its Fountains. London, Macmillan, 1932.
The Avatars, a futurist fantasy. London, Macmillan, 1933.
The House of the Titans, and other poems. London, Macmillan, 1934.
Selected Poems. London, Macmillan, 1935.
The Living Torch. Selections from writings in 'The Irish Statesman', etc., edited, together with an Introductory Essay, by Monk Gibbon. London, Macmillan, 1937.

II

PORTRAITS OF AE

The following 'Iconography' is contributed by Mr. C. P. Curran. It does not claim completeness.

1885–6   Bust, by his fellow-student at the Dublin School of Art, John Hughes, R.H.A. (Municipal Gallery of Modern Art, Dublin).

c. 1902   Portrait in oils. Miss Sarah Purser, R.H.A. (In artist's possession.)

1903   ,,   ,,   John B. Yeats, R.H.A. (Formerly in John Quinn Collection, New York.)

         ,,   ,,   Casimir Dunin Markiewicz (Dublin Municipal Gallery of Modern Art).

1911   Pastel. Mathilde de C. (signed). (F. R. Higgins.)

c. 1914   Portrait in oils. Dermod O'Brien, P.R.H.A. (Abbey Theatre.)

         Self-portrait, Pastel. (Miss Jane Mitchell.)

1914   Drawing in black chalk. Sir W. Rothenstein (published in '24 Drawings, 1st Set').

1916   Bust in marble. Oliver Sheppard, R.H.A. (National Gallery of Ireland.)

         Lithograph, by Mary Duncan.

1921   Drawing. Sir W. Rothenstein (artist's possession).

c. 1924   Wax portrait medallion. T. Spicer Simpson. (Diarmuid Russell.)

A Memoir of AE

c. 1930   Bust. Jerome Connor.
1930   Portrait in oils. Hilda Roberts.
  ,,   ,,   ,,   Estella Solomons.
1933   Bust in bronze. Donald Gilbert.
1935   Two drawings after death. Sean O'Sullivan, R.H.A.
          (1 : Municipal Gallery of Modern Art, Dublin.
          2 : Albert Wood, K.C.)

THE END

www.ingramcontent.com/pod-product-compliance
Lightning Source LLC
Chambersburg PA
CBHW031558110426
42742CB00036B/241